I was drawn to MTN OPS for hunting and fitness—our shared hobbies. When I learned about Trevor's values-based approach to business and his character, I knew we had a lot more in common than just hobbies.

In a landscape where businesses too often choose what is popular over what is right, Trevor's commitment to guide all decision-making through what he calls his Conquer Code (his core values and beliefs) is a breath of fresh air. Similarly, every action we take in my organization (Mayhem Nation) is filtered through our core values: faith, family, fitness, and service.

Trevor has accomplished great things—improving lives, building community and serving the vulnerable. *The Conquer Code* contains wisdom earned from the highs and the lows of his journey, with the hope that you will be inspired to conquer more on your own.

—RICH FRONING, Jr.
CrossFit Games Champion – 4x Individual // 6x Team

Trevor Farnes is one of the finest individuals I have ever known. I cherish my friendship with this inspiring leader. Trevor and Jenna's compelling journey, hardships and all, will challenge anyone who has ever faced obstacles, roadblocks, setbacks, or heartache to carry on, dig deep, and discover one's true capacity, with faith at the center of the efforts. If you want to better connect with your own priorities in life, read *The Conquer Code*. Take notes. Make your own commitments. Follow up on them consistently. And you will accomplish much more of the things that matter most to you. I give this book a Perfect 10!

—PETER VIDMAR
Olympic Gold Medalist and Hall of Fame Speaker

There's so many of us that allow mediocrity to affect our goals and ambitions. Whether it's simply being too lazy to chase your dreams or having a multitude of excuses like having children and claiming there isn't enough time in the day, it's refreshing to see someone like Trevor who not only is one of the most supportive and present fathers I've witnessed, but he is someone who didn't allow the hardships of life to derail him from chasing his dreams and fulfilling them no matter what it took. And never at the cost of his family. I was lucky enough to grow up with a dad who was hyperactive in his children's lives and also chased his dreams and did exactly what he said he would do. In the same vein, Trevor reminds me a lot of my dad's character. Early mornings, late nights and always making time for family is no easy task, but it deserves to be celebrated in a world that so often neglects the importance of being a dad. I'm here to tell you that Trevor deserves to be celebrated and you'll understand this even more so after reading this book and getting a glimpse of the heart and values of not only Trevor but his company as well.

—TRUETT HANES
Guinness Book of World Records Holder

In *The Conquer Code,* Trevor Farnes weaves a captivating narrative that deeply resonates with the spirit of resilience and faith. As a best-selling author and hall of fame speaker, I have encountered countless stories of determination and triumph. However, Farnes' journey stands out for its profound sincerity and the tangible spirituality that courses through every page. This book is more than a testament to overcoming challenges; it's a guide to discovering the Divine in the minutiae of our lives and in the grand expanse of our ambitions.

Farnes masterfully illustrates how everyday moments can lead to monumental growth and understanding, especially when centered on faith and perseverance. His personal story, interlaced with those of individuals like Truett Hanes and insights into the creation of MTN OPS, showcases the power of setting and conquering seemingly insurmountable goals. This is not just a narrative about physical endurance; it's a revelation of the soul's capacity to find strength in the Divine.

As someone who has dedicated my life to inspiring others, I am profoundly touched by *The Conquer Code.* It is a compelling reminder that our most significant conquests come not from external achievements but from the internal journey of faith, love, and relentless pursuit of excellence. Trevor Farnes invites us all to embark on this journey, promising that within its pages lies the blueprint for not only conquering our challenges but also for living a life infused with purpose and divine connection.

I wholeheartedly endorse *The Conquer Code.* Let Trevor Farnes guide you through the seven phases of training in life's marathon, and discover how you, too, can conquer more than you ever thought possible. This book is a must-read for anyone seeking to transform their trials into triumphs through faith, resilience, and the unwavering belief in the power of conquering more.

—CHAD HYMAS

Best-selling author and Hall of Fame speaker

I remember the first time someone told me about MTN OPS. We were in the height of Duck Dynasty, and it was apparent my physical looks were changing. I was 315 pounds and having all sorts of back trouble. I was on daily meds for gout and honestly was just miserable. Then MTN OPS came into my life.

I began taking a daily regimen along with diet modifications and being more active. The pounds started to leave and my joy came back. It was that story that ultimately led to me flying to SLC to finally meet the guy behind the brand. I was in the office 5 mins and knew that Trevor Farnes was my kind of people. His mission was simple, improve the lives of individuals and families, but their goal was tremendous.

I'm glad to say that 10+ years later we are still friends, my 50 pounds have stayed gone, and we are brothers in Christ. *The Conquer Code* takes biblical principles and puts them in a work/life perspective. Now that I have twin boys, I'm so thankful for Trevor and his whole family's willingness to invest in the lives of my children by making me the best I can be here on this Earth. Enjoy this read as we all have and begin to conquer more in your life too! God bless!

—JUSTIN MARTIN

Duck Commander Co, Fin Commander

We often hear of 'inspiring' people, likely allowing it to pass and not sink in. However, we will never forget the people that truly inspire us. Meeting and getting to know Trevor Farnes was one of those moments for me. Trevor's soul force comes from a deep conviction and faith in Jesus Christ, he is a man of purpose with a mission for improving individual lives. Author Jim Collins in his best-seller *Good To Great* talks about level 5 leadership, "A paradoxical combination or personal humility plus professional will." Trevor is a level 5 leader and inspires his team and family with hope to be world changers in a humble sincere manner.

Adversity will happen to us all. It is just past us, you are in it now, or it is on the way. Trials are a part of life for each and every one of us and

The Conquer Code is a must-read for anyone seeking to learn how to struggle well and find triumph on the other side.

—DUSTIN DIEFENDERFER
Founder & CEO of MTNTOUGH Fitness Lab

Trevor is a servant leader who truly understands the way of a conqueror. From the Golden Age of Latin literature we learn that a conqueror is "one who seeks and chooses to be victorious through overcoming adversity and vanquishing fear."

Trevor is a gifted story teller and teacher. At the beginning of the book you'll find a soul-stirring story about how he teaches his four year old daughter Savvy how to seek out and find something that is priceless and precious. This story alone is worth the investment of time and resources required to acquire and read this empowering written work.

What I admire and respect most about Trevor is his understanding of how vital and critical it is to co-create our lives with our Creator. He is truly an inspiring example of a man of faith living and teaching the ways of a conqueror.

One of Trevor's favorite passages from sacred writ dates back to Roman times and eloquently teaches how love will always find a way—"In all these things we are more than conquerors through Him that loved us."

As the Jesuit priest Pierre Teilhard de Chardin taught, "We are not human beings having a spiritual experience; we are spiritual beings having a human experience ... and someday, after mastering the winds, the waves, the tides and gravity, we shall harness for God the energies of love, and then, for a second time in the history of the world, man will have discovered fire." This divine fire, as Trevor so profoundly teaches, is what fuels those who CONQUER.

The Conquer Code will help you discover and understand that you can do more because you were made for more and that it's truly time to start being, having, and doing more.

—KEVIN HALL
International best-selling author of
Aspire: Discovering Your Purpose through the Power of Words.

UNLOCKING SUCCESS THROUGH
FAILURE, FAITH, AND FAMILY

THE CONQUER CODE

TREVOR FARNES

CO-FOUNDER AND CEO OF MTN OPS

FOREWORD BY
CAMERON HANES

Fedd Books
P.O. Box 341973
Austin, TX 78734

www.thefeddagency.com

Published in association with The Fedd Agency, Inc., a literary agency.

ISBN: 978-1-957616-72-8

LCCN: 2024935562

Printed in the United States of America

TABLE OF CONTENTS

FOREWORD:
By Cameron Hanes

Being a blue-collar worker most my life I can always appreciate a success story. I'm not going to lie and say I'm a business man; in fact, I'm the opposite. I often feel overwhelmed and disengaged when it comes to talking business and/or meeting people that are trying to sell me on theirs. With that said, when I met Trevor Farnes through MTN OPS it was the exact opposite. Trevor was humble, authentic, and genuine. You could immediately tell that he was serving a purpose greater than himself and was on a mission to give back to the community.

Working with Trevor for the past 9 years through MTN OPS has been an uplifting experience not only for me but the Keep Hammering Brand. One thing Trevor always says is "They rise highest who lift as they go," and that phrase couldn't be a more accurate description of Trevor's business pursuits. Trevor's vision for the conquer code has been motivating, and what I appreciate is it goes farther then just the physical realm and acknowledges our Lord and Savior Jesus Christ.

As CEO and cofounder of MTN OPS, Trevor has shown remarkable commitment and determination in building a brand that promotes not only physical fitness but also mental resilience and spiritual grounding. His success in this endeavor is a testament to his unwavering dedication and his unique ability to lead and inspire others.

I am thankful for the opportunity to write this foreword for Trevor Farnes, someone who has dedicated his life to empowering others to become the best version of themselves. So grab this book, take up the challenge, and commit to conquering more in all aspects of life.

Stay focused, stay dedicated, and keep hammering!

AUTHOR'S NOTE

The sun burst through the windows on an early Sunday morning. My wife and four children were all sound asleep. Peace filled our home. I woke with excitement in my soul and a desire to dive into the scriptures while the house was still quiet. To me there was no greater way to start my day, especially on the Sabbath.

I left my bedroom and headed to my home office. As I walked down the hall, little Savvy, who was four years old at the time, came out of her room and ran past me toward the kitchen. That's when a very distinct impression and words filled my heart and mind:

> *"While she is still young and learning to read, you can still teach her to find names of God in the scriptures."*

Feeling moved, I told Savvy to grab her scriptures, a copy her grandparents had given her in the first year of life, and to meet me in my office. When she came in, I took a little colored sticky note and wrote on it the names "Lord, God, Jesus," and I then gave her a red pencil and said, "I want you to open your scriptures and find these names. When you do, I want you to circle them with the red pencil." She studied the three names, opened the pages of her scriptures, and went to work like she would with a *Where's Waldo* book.

Then, with excitement in her voice and all over her face, she said, "Dad, I found 'Lord'!" and circled it. We were both so happy about her discovery. She looked at me with a questioning look as if to ask, "Now what?"

So, I told her, "Let's see if you can find Him again."

She flipped the page and, with even greater amazement, said, "I found the Lord again!" We were both even more thrilled than the first time, and she went back to work. Just a moment later, I heard "I found the Lord again." With that, she began to focus on the word "Lord," and she continued to find Him on every page of the book.

Savvy followed this pattern until it was time to go to church, but she did not stop there. As we sat in the congregation that day and for the entire hour of that worship service, every few minutes, she would lean over to me with her continued expression of success and joy to share in a whisper, "I found The Lord again!" This ended up being the best babysitting tool to keep her and the other kids quiet during church that we had ever found.

Upon arriving home, Savvy's seeking continued and seemed to pick up more and more momentum throughout the day. When dinner time was upon us, she sat with her plate of food in front of her, but her scripture feast also sat to one side. She did not cease eating up all that she could from her search for some of the most sacred and fulfilling words known to man.

As she continued to blurt out, "I found the Lord again," our family laughed at every encounter but also recognized the profound learning that was transpiring within the heart and life of this precious four-year-old.

As night came, I tucked Savvy into her bed, kissed her forehead, and expressed my love for her. She then asked me, "Dad, do you want me to do this every day?"

With all the emotion I could share from the feelings of a tender parent, I replied, "Yes, Savvy! I want you to find the Lord again and again and again every day of your life."

What powerful truths and wisdom our little children can teach us. I begin with this story to testify that if we choose to, we can and will "Find The Lord Again" and again on all the pages of our lives. If we choose to have eyes to see and hearts to feel, we will continue to find Him.

I want to take a moment to express that I understand, revere, and honor that people have different names, descriptions, and ideas for their source of creation, strength, energy, and comfort. I readily acknowledge this reality. My source is the Lord, Jesus Christ, and I am a devoted member of The Church of Jesus Christ of Latter-Day Saints. When I write about *The Conquer Code*, ultimately, I write about Jesus Christ being the code. With the connections made through business and personal life, I have been blessed to work with and become close to people from all walks of life, backgrounds, and beliefs, many of whom have asked that I share my story. With mutual respect and understanding for the varying beliefs, I will be open, bold, and honest about the beauty of my beliefs and readily acknowledge the beauty of others as well.

As the author of this book, it is my prayer that you will Find The Lord Again on each page of this book, in each of my stories shared, in all that you might feel, and especially as you ponder your own life stories. In the end, my ultimate desire, my mission in life, and the reason I am writing in the first place is to recognize God and, in some way, awaken the Divine with *all* who read these words. This is how we conquer.

INTRODUCTION

In 2020, amidst the chaos of Covid, I witnessed greatness inside our corporate gym at our headquarters in Fruit Heights, Utah. My company, MTN OPS, had just hired Truett Hanes from Oregon. Truett is the son of Cam Hanes, an MTN OPS ambassador who happened to be a legend in the hunting and running community. He was known for never letting excuses get in the way of his success, both physically and mentally.

The Hanes family never seemed to back away from a good challenge; instead, they ran to it. What Truett was up to was a good example of their relentless approach to life. Truett had decided to take it upon himself to break a David Goggins record. Goggins was a world-famous ultramarathon runner, ultra-distance cyclist, triathlete, and retired Navy Seal. He held a record for the greatest number of pull-ups in a twenty-four-hour period. Goggins's record at the time was 4,030 in seventeen hours and eight minutes—absolutely mind blowing to me! *How in the world will Truett Hanes conquer that?* I couldn't help but wonder.

My family visited Truett in the gym that day, and while he cranked out five pull-ups every thirty seconds or so, my four kids and wife and I held colorful signs that declared, "You Can Do It, Truett!" It was incredible to watch—and painful. We saw his hands already becoming torn to shreds, literally battle-beaten, blistered, and bleeding. My wife and children's faces were filled with compassion, and yet, every thirty seconds Truett held onto that bar and pulled himself up and hoisted his chin over and over until he had done *4,100 pull-ups within about the same time—seventy over Goggins record!* I was super excited for him and so grateful that my children were there to be inspired by someone pushing themselves beyond what they had ever done before.

On one of his breaks during this incredible feat, I chatted with Truett for just a moment. Watching a record being broken, I suddenly felt inspired to do something more physically challenging than I had ever done before. I also felt inspired to request that Truett challenge me to do something great right then and there. I told him so.

Truett immediately responded, "Run a marathon, Trevor. Less than 1 percent of the world population has ever run a marathon."

I looked him in the eyes. "Challenge accepted."

Something about witnessing greatness within individuals has always inspired and motivated me to do more. Watching my children witness the example of someone conquering their unknown was equally powerful. It urged me to be that same kind of example to them. A desire to physically show them that we as humans are capable of pushing ourselves to greater limits than we often do surged within me. I went to work.

We all know that "misery loves company," and with my fortieth birthday coming up, I thought it would be a great idea to celebrate with some suffering! So, I invited friends and family to join me in this challenge to conquer more. I somehow enticed close to thirty of my closest friends, coworkers, and family members into suffering with me . . . to train and run a marathon. It would be *incredible*!

Some say forty is mid-life, but since I plan on living to 100, I was not quite there. Still, because forty was a big year, I wanted it to be different and memorable. The longest races I had ever run before were multiple 5K (three mile) races. I'd suffered with knee issues for years, but those were gone now, due to surgery and physical therapy. Even then, I had typically run those 5Ks while pushing a stroller, one of our children enjoying the ride. Yes, while I loved being with my four children, truthfully, the stroller had acted as a walker to lean on during those arduous (for me) three-mile runs.

Realization dawned. I was going to have to up my game.

Thinking this would be a one-and-done event, I set out to find the hardest marathon I could possibly find within a reasonable distance from my home. Living in Utah, where the outdoors is a popular passion, I didn't need to look far. The Moab Trail Marathon in southern Utah could provide a challenge none of the thirty running with me had ever faced or endured physically, and because of this, I knew it was the right one. Plus, the Moab Trail Marathon just happened to land on the week of my fortieth birthday. Bonus!

On the race website, it boldly claimed the title of "Mother of All Trail Marathons" and "Bucket List" race by Trail Runner Magazine. But what made it such a race? The terrain was demanding, and inclines seemed to be around every corner.

I'd maneuvered rough terrain before . . . at least in life, where the climb, the obstacle, the mountain in my way seemed unclimbable, feeling that the odds were stacked against me day in and day out. There were some times in my life when I felt pain, despair, and loneliness so great that I could not see the summit because I was far too deep in what felt like a crater that I kept sinking deeper and deeper into.

In those hardest moments, I gratefully took the courage to do a little more each and every day—a little more spiritually, a little more physically, a little more mentally, and a little more socially. A little more was all I had, but a little more made all the difference. Taking small and steady steps up and over the obstacles, I was blessed with strength that built my confidence and brought to my remembrance all that was divine within me.

I became the CEO and Co-Founder of MTN OPS, which launched in July of 2014. A small handful of people I respect and admire came together to form a *highly differentiated* company. Each of them, like me, had experienced their own business and other life marathons with mountains of obstacles, and that training brought wisdom we shared together. We also took a hard look around at the world we lived in. Out there, we noticed hatred, division, competition, complacency, depression, struggle, poverty, and spiritual poverty. We wanted to somehow address that, too.

You see, we had an extraordinary product I'd developed to transform lives. We knew on that foundation we *could* simply create an energy and nutritional company of amazing products, or **we could create an entire *community*,** improving the lives of countless individuals and families by inspiring them to achieve their best, increase their confidence, and provide hope. Ultimately, we could connect and conquer.

Together, we made a choice. Since then, I could not be prouder of this company! MTN OPS grew to not only offer the highest quality energy and performance products backed by science but also created a unique community to unify all of us in our journey to Conquer More: spiritually, physically, mentally, and socially. And it happened. Based on these sound principles of challenge and service, the company rapidly grew and continues to grow.

The spirit of conquering more was exactly what I needed as I prepared for "The Mother of All Trail Marathons." Not to minimize other marathons, but it truly was a different beast with its incredibly rugged, remote, and unforgiving terrain. I was bound and determined to not only run it but to run it well by training specifically and consistently over a determined period.

My training started at the base of the Matterhorn Mountain in Switzerland with world-famous ultra-marathoner Tommy Rivers Puzey! This was via my iFit App on the treadmill in my basement. Yeah, I made that sound cool, like I was really going big, but I started on a treadmill. I just happened to be looking on the app for a trainer, found a man who, for some reason, looked familiar, clicked on his impressive profile, and then started following him up the Matterhorn on my very first trail run in the basement of my home. I was hooked.

Something about Tommy and the way he taught along the trail spoke to me but also sounded familiar. I reached out to him via Instagram to thank him for being a great virtual trainer, not expecting a person of his notoriety to respond, but he did. His words were humble, kind, and encouraging.

I did not know, as we messaged back and forth, that Tommy was actually lying in a hospital bed, death knocking on his door as he battled a rare form of lung cancer. While he faced a much more threatening mountain than I was facing on the treadmill, he took time to respond and to lift where he stood. In other words, he lifted where he laid.

One message from Tommy, just about a week into our conversations, came by way of a voice message. His tone was slow and raspy, and he apologized for not having sent a text but mentioned that his thumbs were not working that day. He was too tired and worn out to move any of his fingers, yet he took the time to send me a voice message. His encouragement made my running that much more meaningful. While he was known around the world for his physical feats, maybe I could run a few extra miles for him while he physically could not for himself.

As the weather improved and it was time to move out to the real mountains, Tommy introduced me to his brother Jacob, who was living in Canada and training runners virtually. Right away, I hired him as my coach to guide me through the process of building for my marathon. I did not hire a coach to help me win *the* race, but I did hire a coach to help me win *my* race, and it made all the difference. Training works. Starting strong and building from one phase to another and another is vital.

Writing this book was a lot like preparing to run my first marathon. This, too, was a first for me, and while not quite the physical challenge the marathon was, this was a challenge of mental, physical, and spiritual exertion on my part. It was years in the making.

Just like the physical preparation for my marathon, there were waves of excitement, "highs," and times when everything just flowed. On the other hand, it seemed there were far greater times when I struggled, suffering some "lows." I doubted whether the efforts were worth it, if anyone would even care to read my words. The emotions that came while writing were different but similar to all those experienced in my race preparation and even race day.

One thing was very similar in training for both experiences. It was my family waiting at the end.

During my race training, even on short runs, I would get caught up in the emotion of imagining my wife and children standing at the finish line, waiting to greet me with open arms. That moment in Moab is one I will always remember, and it was their faces that inspired me to keep moving forward to the race completion.

Race day was upon us. The countdown began, and we were off. The first four miles headed up through a picturesque red rock canyon, and the adrenaline of the event seemed to pump through my veins as I climbed. Mile fourteen presented two straight miles of what felt like a relentless incline. Compared to most races, there were not many aid stations. Yes, there were enough but not very frequent, so packing a few essentials was just that: *essential.*

In my opinion, in many races, the roar of the crowd, the consistent cheers, and shouts from the spectators can have a positive impact on your performance. In the Moab Trail Marathon, however, it was so beautiful but so remote that spectators were only allowed at the finish line. It required a different mental strength to keep yourself and the runners around you motivated and positive as we confronted the challenging terrain that surrounded us.

As I prepared for the race, I wrote down twenty-six names, one for every mile my feet would cover. I also made a playlist of songs provided to me by the people on that list. Each mile was dedicated to them, and each mile a song or two played in my head and heart as I ran for that person. I started the race running the first mile, covering a gradual incline.

The first couple of songs were from my wife, Jenna. "Heart of Courage," from the *Invincible* soundtrack, rang true to me. I felt like I had gained precisely that by training for that day. "You Are the Reason," by Calum Scott, came next. When I listened to it and thought of her, it brought a great sweat to my eyes. She is incredible and always worth running for.

I then ran for each of my children, my parents, and my seven siblings. I ran for Tommy, who was not able to run. I ran for my team at MTN OPS. I ran for Mason Ferrulli, a young man with a true Heart of Courage as he faced cancer at such a young age. The song he provided me with was "Gonna Know We Were Here" by Jason Aldean.

Can you imagine the tears that rolled down my face as I listened to Mason's song, knowing the suffering he was facing, truly facing his own mountain—cancer. The message from that song of not knowing where we might be in twenty years, but the world would surely know Mason was here. To you, Mason, we know you are here, and you are going to be here for a long time. Thank you for blessing us all with your heart and life of courage. You were made to conquer, my friend.

There was one moment toward the end of the marathon on the desert trail that I will never forget. Staring at the path ahead of me, with my feet pounding forward on the red earth, I noticed that it looked like the race was coming to an end. In fact, I could see the finish line; I could hear the announcer, and the crowd was energized. It was just what I needed!

But as I got closer, my watch told me I still had just over three miles left. *What?* It felt like a little game the race engineers played just to get in my head right at the end. For a moment, the course passed the finish line area, so I heard my family cheering my name.

Psyche! Thirty seconds later, I was left to my own inner thoughts: *how in the world do I put one more foot in front of the other? And why does it feel like I am running uphill this entire time?*

Not only did the mental challenge really kick in, but the race purveyors added a ladder climb up a cliff side and two areas where ropes were required to climb up and repel down! That made the physical challenge that much more grueling.

Those grueling last three miles. Those were for God. During that physical journey, man, did I need Him then, just like in the other tough times in my life. His strength carried me across that finish line to my family who were constantly in my mind and heart, waiting there to greet me. When I gathered the last of my strength and ran up the last thirty-yard incline, I met a plateau. That was where everyone waited, and at the top were my parents, my mom with her signature excitement and cheer.

I heard the announcer share my name and I saw their faces—the ones who are my life's breath, who kept me smiling throughout the race: Jenna, Hallie, Kenzie, Beckham, and Savvy. My arms went up to the sky. I crossed the line!

I had finished my race, and they were my reward.

The emotions ran freely, but so did the exhaustion and some pain. I literally sat there thinking, *how can anyone go any further?* I had once thought the same about a marathon and now my question shifted dramatically: *how much farther can I go?*

And here's the thing: with a reward like mine across the finish line, there is no telling how far I might go. From that day on, I was officially ready to Conquer More.

My greatest hope is that many will benefit from this book's pages, but in the end, I see my wife and my children benefiting from its completion, waiting with open arms to receive what I have wrestled to finish. After all, they know I do it for them. I wrote this book for and to my wife and children and my children's children, and I do so with *one* goal in mind. In my book, I will "Talk of Christ," I will "Rejoice in Christ," and I will "Preach of Christ." I will do all this so that my children may know the true source of strength to CONQUER this life (2 Nephi 25:26, emphasis added).

I wrote this so that my children might look unto Jesus as the "Author and Finisher of my faith" and that of theirs. (Moroni 6:4)

To you, the person looking to find hope, strength, and confidence to do more and be more, I pray that my thoughts and experiences shared might strike a chord with you in your own life. We all have much to learn, and if not by our own experiences, by the experiences of others. I hope that some simple truths I have come to know might be meaningful in your pursuit to conquer.

I promise that through the pages of my book, and if you look closely enough at the pages *of your life's book,* you will find the path to conquer more in life. So, let's talk, in black and white, about what that process of conquering more is going to look like.

We're going to break this down into seven phases (aka chapters) of training to align with the strong metaphor of the training I just went through to prepare for my marathon. The number seven has significance. In the Bible, seven often symbolizes completion or perfection. While this book is far from perfect, I love the symbolism and the process we go through in life toward that ultimate end.

To share how I conquer in life, I'll happily and honestly walk you through some of my life's journey.

Phase 1 (BUILD THE FOUNDATION) will start by sharing stories and experiences from my childhood and teenage years to demonstrate the kind of incredible parenting that occurred in my home and the foundational impact that has had throughout my life.

Phase 2 (BUILD STRENGTH TO ENDURE) will share stories and experiences from a two-year service mission I completed for my church.

Phase 3 (BUILD FOR SPEED) will share stories and experiences, including my love story with my wife, Jenna, and the blessing of becoming parents to four incredible children (Hallie, Kenzie, Beckham, and Savvy).

Phase 4 (BUILT TO CONQUER) will share stories and experiences from some difficult financial times for our family. It's vital for you, my reader, to understand what it took to endure and then Conquer these seemingly unclimbable mountains.

Phase 5 (BUILD TO BREATHE) will share stories and experiences of coming out of those financial struggles together as a family and how it was made possible for us to succeed and breathe again.

Phase 6 (BUILD FOR THE HUNT) will share stories and experiences as the pioneer of hunting in my family and what that time and attention with loved ones in the outdoors has come to mean to me.

Phase 7 (BUILT TO CONQUER MORE) will share stories and experiences of conquering in life by following "THE CON-

QUER CODE."

You may notice that in each of these phases, I will share stories and experiences. God has given me personal experiences that have strengthened me. I firmly believe that He has given me these specific stories and experiences to bless someone. Maybe even you. The perspective these experiences have afforded me is priceless. That is why it is my hope through sharing that you will observe that your life and a great, benevolent power can afford you a similar perspective. There is a lot of power in choosing to be open, so I invite you to choose to have eyes to see and hearts to feel what God will place before you.

The greatest Teacher of us all also wrote in parables and stories. His teachings were simple enough for even someone like me to understand, yet deep enough to leave you fed and wanting more. I don't pretend to teach like the Savior, but I do strive to teach in the Savior's way. I, like all of us, am a work in progress, just like a marathon.

In my seven months of training prior to my Moab Marathon, I would run five to six times per week, anywhere from four to eighteen miles per day. The days of our lives might often feel like some of these grueling runs, as not all are easy. I would often look ahead in the distance to some object or monument, sometimes a tree, sometimes a rock, and I would give all I had until I reached that predetermined mark. Upon arriving at that spot, I would choose another marked object, giving my all until I arrived there again.

One day, as I neared the end of my marathon training, I pondered this way of progressing through my runs: looking ahead to something in the distance, not being in the moment where I actually and physically was. Yes, it kept me going and moving forward, so it was not all bad. But as I look at how these runs paralleled life, I to this day remind myself to stop looking "beyond the mark."

The "mark" I refer to is our Savior, Jesus Christ. Never is He beyond the mark, too far off in the distance; never is He something too far out of our reach. He is always present and always near. Personally, He is my source of strength, peace, and courage to carry on, to move forward despite all odds.

He is how I conquer.

Are you ready to conquer with me? Let's go!

NOW IS THE TIME TO AWAKEN THE DIVINE

There's an old Hindu legend about a time when all human beings were Gods. But they so abused their divinity that Brahma, the Chief God, decided to take it away from them and hide their godliness in a place where it could never be found. In order to find the best spot, however, he needed to hold a council of the Gods to help him decide.

"Let's bury it deep in the earth," said the Gods.

Brahma answered, "No, that will not do, because humans will dig into the earth and find it."

The Gods replied, "Okay, let's sink it in the deepest ocean then."

But Brahma said, "No, not there, for they will learn to dive, and they will find it."

Then the Gods said, "What about the highest mountain top, out in the farthest corner of the earth?"

But again Brahma replied, "No, that will not do either, because they will eventually climb every mountain, scale every peak, search every hidden cave, and once again find and take up their divinity."

The rest of the Gods were exasperated. They threw up their arms in surrender. "There is no place!" they hollered. "The humans will proliferate, and they will find it anywhere we put it."

Brahma was quiet for a time. He thought long and deep. Finally, he looked up at the rest of the Gods, a knowing twinkle in his eye. "Here is what we shall do," he said. "We will hide their divinity deep down in the one place they will surely never look—the very center of their own being."

The rest of the Gods rejoiced. Of course! It was the perfect place! They all formally agreed on it, and the deed was done.

Ages passed, and since then, humans have been on a desperate and unending search, traveling every corner of the planet, digging, diving, climbing, and exploring—searching for the one thing they know they've lost and just can't seem to find.

To me, this legend leaves with it a great thought and principle that we do have a divine nature. Each and every one of us is a divine creation. Because of the conviction that I have gained in my own life of the reality of a supreme Creator, with us as His children, it is my desire to *awaken* the divine within the individuals I am blessed to cross paths with on this journey of life.

PHASE 1
BUILD THE FOUNDATION

"Therefore whosoever heareth these sayings of mine, and doeth them, I will liken him unto a wise man, which built his house upon a rock:

And the rain descended, and the floods came, and the winds blew, and beat upon that house; and it fell not: for it was founded upon a rock.

And ever one that heareth these saying of mine, and doeth them not, shall be likened unto a foolish man, which built his house upon the sand:

And the rain descended, and the floods came, and the winds blew, and beat upon that house: and it fell: and great was the fall of it."

—MATTHEW 7:24-27

A wise man or woman will always build upon a solid foundation whether that be for things physical or spiritual. I believe that all things in life are first built spiritually and then physically. I believe God first created all things spiritually before the physical creation was brought about, just like any action (physical) first being preceded by a thought or idea (spiritual). But when it came to my marathon training, I had to build upon foundational principles, just as all athletes must do in order to grow.

While there may be mentors, trainers, and types of hacks, in reality there are no shortcuts to truly conquering. This mindset of building a foundation in life both physically and spiritually must be obeyed and respected to avoid costly mistakes, injury, delay, and major disappointment.

What this looked like for marathon preparation was starting slowly, allowing my feet, legs, and lungs an opportunity to acclimate to the new pressure they were put under. This took patience, and I'm not always a patient man. It looked like improvement with my nutrition, sleep, and hydration. It took planning and not just for myself but for my family who would also be affected by my new physical regimen. There is much that goes into building upon a foundation, but when the wind blows and the rain falls, a strong and sure foundation will make all the difference.

I have literally seen this prediction with the wise and foolish man play out before my eyes. As a family, we travel to Lake Powell every year and love the memories made in that beautiful creation. It can be one of the most incredibly peaceful places on earth and one of the most hectic places to travel! Each trip requires a lot of manpower, all hands on deck, and a willingness from its passengers to get their hands a little wet and dirty. This especially rings true when it comes to securing the seventy-five-foot-long houseboat our family has owned a timeshare in for the past eight years to either rock or sand, in hopes that you have anchored yourself to weather any storm that may come your way . . . and trust me, they *will* come your way.

Through experience, both good and bad, my entire family and sometimes friends, usually thirty-plus people on the boat, have found that anchoring to giant rocks both on the front and back ends of the boat allowed us to withstand even the strongest winds, waves, and storms.

I recall one night as we sat well-anchored to our rocks amidst a storm, watching from a distance as many nearby houseboats that had chosen to anchor into the sand were coming loose.

The passengers aboard these houseboats were holding flashlights, frantically leaping from their boats to re-dig and re-burry anchors as deeply into the sand on the shores of the lake as possible. They had to work ceaselessly all night until the winds ceased to keep their boats from floating out into the water or up against the incredible and dangerous cliffsides that surrounded them.

As we watched, these words of a wise man building upon a rock came to mind, and my group and I were grateful that we were all able to confront the raging storm with peace and confidence because of the rock upon which we were anchored.

A favorite scripture of mine states, "Remember, remember that it is upon the rock of our Redeemer, who is Christ, the Son of God, that ye must build your foundation; that when the devil shall send forth his mighty winds, yea, his shafts in the whirlwind, yea, when all his hail and his mighty storm shall beat upon you, it shall have no power over you to drag you down to the gulf of misery and endless wo, because of the rock upon which ye are built, which is a sure foundation, a foundation whereon if men build they cannot fall" (Helaman 5:12).

THE FIRST MILES

Coming into this world was not an easy task for me, not that I remember. But my mother tells me often of the marathon it was during labor and delivery to make sure I made it alive and healthy.

Fast-forward twenty years from my difficult birth. I was serving in Mexico as a missionary for my church. I was asked to be the trainer that day on a particular subject, and so I completed my teaching in front of the chapel containing about thirty missionaries. Upon sitting back in my seat, grateful to have that assignment completed, they invited the mission physician, Dr. Jones from Utah, to stand and train us on health and wellness.

Before the doctor started, he looked straight at me and said, "Farnes . . . Your parents don't happen to be Gary and Mary Farnes, do they?"

I sat up straight in my chair, feeling the eyes of thirty other young missionaries turn toward me. "Yes," I responded slowly, "those are my parents."

Silence held as I watched the doctor appear to calculate something in his head. "If my memory serves me well and with your age, you must be their child who was born as an emergency C-Section?"

With wide eyes, I replied, "Yes, that was me."

He grinned, "Your father and I prayed over you and your mother, right before I performed that emergency operation that brought you into this world. I was your mother's doctor." He paused again, and, his eyes moist, he said, "What we just witnessed of you speaking here today was a miracle. The fact that you are here is a miracle to me."

I sat there in amazement that, of all places, there in Mexico stood the doctor who not only delivered me but who, by the guidance of God, knew when and how to perform the procedure to deliver me in a healthy state. The umbilical cord had been wrapped around my neck for a prolonged period—not enough to kill me, but enough to leave me brain dead.

We are one of one, not one of a thousand, a million, or even a trillion. We are each unique, and that should be recognized as a gift. Paulo Coelho once said, "In a forest of a hundred thousand trees, no two leaves are alike. And no two journeys along the same path are alike."

With this in mind, imagine growing up in a home where you *felt loved just like that*—like an "unrepeatable miracle." That was the home I grew up in. I know not everyone is afforded the same blessing and security of a safe and peaceful home, but for whatever reason, I was. And I bless my parents for creating such a rare place for me and my six siblings to grow up in.

As a young kid, I had many fears, and as I look back upon my childhood, I recognize the extreme separation anxiety that existed. Being apart from my family scared me; the thought of the death of a loved one terrified me, and even the thought of leaving home to attend kindergarten was more than I could bear.

Because of this, I will always be eternally grateful that my parents focused our family's attention on being Together Forever. There was nothing I wanted more than this. I was part of a family; I had parents who lived with extreme intention, and this intention and belonging were exactly what my troubled mind needed.

I have often wondered why I was born with such anxieties and to be honest, I don't have all the answers. I do believe that we are born with our own personality traits and one of mine is a need to feel secure with the ones I love. I *also* believe that life's events can cause these emotions that we may already naturally have to be enhanced.

One event in my childhood that only enhanced my separation anxiety happened when I was in third grade. School was out for the day, and my parents had given my younger brother Trent and me permission to go play at my friend Brian's house right after school. We were a group of five young boys, excited to be out of school and ready to go explore and play; all of us, either on a bike or a skateboard, headed toward Brian's home.

It was a nice warm day; the kind kids love. As we traveled down the tree-lined street only a few blocks away from the school and just a block away from Brian's house, I saw a car pull over in the distance, and a man jumped out of the passenger door. I remember the exact scene. The details of what transpired are engraved in my memory. That man went around the car, across the street, and started walking down the sidewalk across the street from us. He never really looked our way but kept his focus directly in front of him.

As I watched the guy walk up the sidewalk, I had a sudden feeling that something was suspicious about him. He didn't look at us until he was directly across the street from where we were. At that point, he abruptly turned in our direction and began to run toward us.

"What are you doing?" I cried, confused and scared. "What are you doing?"

He never responded and never said a word, which made him all the more frightening to us young boys. He grabbed me by the arm, which was terrifying. Suddenly, my younger brother Trent started hitting the man with his skateboard with all his might. Indelibly imprinted on my mind was the abject fear on each of our faces while we yelled at the man in confusion.

Still gripping my arm, the man then tried to grab another one of our friends. As he did, I noticed the driver inside the car now driving up quickly as if ready to take us and drive off.

Fortunately, none of the kids ran away, and there were enough of us to resist, fight back, and cause commotion—enough to not make us an easy target for them. Frustrated, the man jumped back into the car empty-handed. They sped off as we all frantically rode to Brian's home, where his mother called the police, and we anxiously waited for the officer to arrive.

My young heart, already sensitive, relived this event over and over again in my mind, wondering what could have happened. I was eternally grateful for the safe outcome in what I knew full well by the looks on those men's faces would have been a tragic event.

In all honesty, I am not sure what those two men truly planned to do that day. Were they just trying to scare us? Or were they really going to do us harm? None of us knew anything except how frightening it had been in the moment. The event was reported to my elementary school where the next day I was asked to stand in front of a body of students to let them know the exact details of what had happened to warn other kids and families in the neighborhood to beware.

The fact that the school asked me to do this created an even more intense feeling of the reality of what happened. It put my troubled heart in an even more heightened state of fear. I now feared leaving home most days, always watching and wondering the intent of adults around me. I feared every time I was left alone, even if a babysitter was there. I was afraid when my mother would leave for an activity or even to run errands.

Looking back, I realize I could not have been the easiest child to raise because of the daily anxieties I faced. In fact, I slept on my parents' floor until I was almost twelve years old. I was the sixth of seven children. Despite this and their busy schedules, my parents were patient, loving, and kind to me and all my siblings, each of us with our unique talents and challenges.

Now as an adult, I hope I can be half of what my parents were to me. I hope to offer the same patience and loving care to my children, who are being raised in a world full of fear and anxiety.

I have a mother who, for my entire kindergarten year, walked me to school and then sat out on the playground, allowing my brother to play while I would run to the school window every fifteen to twenty minutes to make sure she was still there. She always was. After our street attack by those men, she helped me move past that, too. She knew my needs, and she sacrificed to make sure I could grow. I did grow out of this and improved, but it was, as they say, "slowly but surely."

I have a father who left early for work each day and taught me the value of hard work through his example. Not only did he work hard to make a living, but he also accepted, as did my mother, any assignment in our church for service and did so with a humble and willing heart. My father held many leadership roles within work and church and presided in our home as a father should. He was not much of an outdoorsman, but when I turned twelve and joined the Boy Scouts, I was so grateful when he was asked to serve as the Scout Master in our local area.

He accepted, and my anxious heart rested in knowing that my dad would be on every campout I would go on. Both of us being novice outdoorsmen, we made the most of every campout, every month for two years straight. We saw incredible sights, explored amazing mountains, and even dug and slept in our own ice cave. My love for the outdoors grew as my father and I spent more time together in it. My relationship with my father also grew as I realized I could always count on him to be there for me, especially in situations where my anxieties would normally skyrocket.

TOOLS TO BUILD A FOUNDATION FOR LIFE

As I mentioned, my parents raised us with true intention, always seeking to teach us, take care of us, and recognize the good we did in the world. They made life's events special for each of us. Being an intentional parent—or being an intentional person, for that matter—is not easy. Intentionality requires a lot of effort, but as a result, it will yield the greatest results in the lives of those with whom you choose to be intentional, creating bonds that last forever.

In a proclamation from my church leaders to the world about "THE FAMILY," there are some powerful words that read:

> *"Happiness in family life is most likely to be achieved when founded upon the teachings of the Lord Jesus Christ. Successful marriages and families are established and maintained on principles of faith, prayer, repentance, forgiveness, respect, love, compassion, work, and wholesome recreational activities."*

My parents were intentional in so many ways, always turning us to the Lord Jesus Christ, teaching us principles of His gospel, helping us learn the value of hard work, and also providing us with fun-filled family activities that brought us together. I want to list a few simple ideas and examples that I feel can be great takeaways for parents or future parents.

These examples may be simple answers to questions about how we can live the most beneficial and intentional life. But to me, while being simple, they represent the most sacred and fundamental answers to life's questions about how to build upon and stay planted on a firm foundation.

At a very young age I had a firm foundation in these four facts:

- I knew that there was a God.
- I knew He not only wanted to hear from me, but I found through experience at a young age that He also answered my prayers and wanted me to hear Him!
- I knew that my relationship with God was that of Him being my Father in Heaven and I was His son. I learned that nothing in life will bring peace and confidence such as this.
- As I built upon this foundation and relationship, I knew that God had a plan for me, that I could communicate with Him along the pathway of this plan, during the good and the bad, and that He would direct my path.

To my children and to you, the reader, I hope and pray that you discover this same relationship in your own life. I challenge you to spend time on your knees in communion with a God who knows you, loves you, and desires for you to one day return home to Him.

TOOL #1: PRAYER

Never did I leave my childhood home without kneeling in prayer with either my father or mother or both. I heard them pray for me by name each and every day, asking God to protect and watch over me as I tried to make decisions that would keep me close to Him.

Never did I go to bed without having knelt with my family as we thanked God for the blessings of that day and for protection to be upon us while we slept.

Never did I eat a meal that was not prayed over in our home.

If you were a friend of mine growing up, you might have heard more prayers than you'd have liked while visiting the Farnes' home. But my parents pleaded with and thanked God in all ways and for all things.

A passage of scripture that comes to mind as I think of my home while growing up states: *"That your incomings may be in the name of the Lord, that your outgoings may be in the name of the Lord, that all your salutations may be in the name of the Lord, with uplifted hands unto the Most High. . ." (Doctrine and Covenants 109:9).*

As a young child, I played many sports, but my favorites were soccer and football. Before any game, my mother would ask if I had gone to my room to pray for God's help. With this gentle reminder, I got into a beautiful habit of kneeling at my bedside before any athletic game through my high school years.

When our team once lost a football game and I made my way back to the car, defeated, my mother said, "Remember to say a prayer of thanks to Heavenly Father once you arrive home."

"We lost, Mom, so why should I pray?"

She looked at me with compassion and sincerity. "We give thanks to God in *all* things, even on days we lose, so that *we can always find good in the bad...* that is what we should thank God for."

Soon, I realized that even the ability to be out on that field playing was reason enough to take a moment to thank Him. With that, I got into another beautiful habit as a kid of returning home after every game and again kneeling at my bedside, no matter the outcome of the game, to give thanks to a God who gave me the air to breathe and many other abilities while out on the field that day.

This habit bled into many other areas of my life as my relationship with my Father in Heaven grew. This relationship and ability to turn to Him in *all* aspects of life has been so critical for the foundation that my parents were helping me to build upon.

TOOL #2: SCRIPTURE STUDY

Never did the scriptures rest in our home. Just like with prayer, we didn't always like it as children. But did my siblings and I come to recognize the power and strength that comes from them both as we have matured? Yes!

My parents were intentional in gathering us together on a regular basis as a family to read in the scriptures. They obtained scripture videos that, as children, we could watch to better understand the stories on a simpler level in the understanding of a child.

When my parents gathered us for our Family Night every Monday, they would teach us a simple message from the scriptures.

They taught us the power of the scriptures by opening them to us on a regular basis and challenging us to read them on our own as often as possible. In Phase 7, I will share how this has become a lifelong habit and pursuit that has blessed and changed my life immensely.

Taking time to open the words of God is like opening a "letter from home," as my mom always expresses, and allows us to hear the words God would guide and direct us with.

TOOL #3: FAMILY NIGHT

Family time was not "all the time," but my parents were intentional in their pursuit to make sure family time was a regular priority in our home.

Monday night from 6-8 p.m. or so was Family Night in our home. In all my years, not much could interfere with this! We would have dinner, some type of activity, and spiritual thought to go along with the evening. If, for some reason, there was a conflict that could not be altered on Monday night, my parents were so committed to us as a family that they made sure to hold our Family Night on Sunday evening. But it always took place.

Do you have a Family Night tradition in your home that your children can count on? If not, I challenge you to create your Family Night, a time when your family—no matter its size—can experience safety, peace, and recreational activity with the family. God has blessed you to enjoy this journey of life.

TOOL #4: SERVICE

Do your children see you serve? Do they catch you in the act of greatness as you attend to the needs of others?

My parents taught me that we don't serve to be seen, but I am eternally grateful that I saw them serve and love others. Service was commonplace in our home and in my life. I now love the word "charity," which is the pure love of Christ. If any two beings in my life embodied charity to me as I grew up, it was my parents.

Around 2010, I read a book that changed my life. The author Kevin Hall, who I have now come to know and who has become a great friend and mentor of mine, teaches a secret word in his book *Aspire: Discovering Your Purpose Through the Power of Words*. That word is **Genshai.** It means to "never do anything that would make a person feel small, *including yourself*." He then goes on to teach that if you are to give a needy person a coin on the street, don't just hand it to them and walk away. Instead, kneel down, place it in their hand, look them in the eyes, and allow them to feel and see your genuine concern and love. Living this way, you would be considered a practitioner of Genshai—or that pure love, charity.

I once sat in the congregation at my church with my mother and my younger brother when I was seventeen years old. At this point in my life, we had moved to Washington, D.C. to serve a mission for our church as a family. That particular Sunday was referred to as a Fast and Testimony Sunday in our church, where the members of the congregation held a fast and were allowed to go up to the pulpit to share their personal feelings and testimonies of the gospel.

My father was visiting another congregation, as he often did as part of his service at the time and was not with us that day. Still, as we sat there, a gentleman from our congregation approached the pulpit and expressed that he wanted to share an incredible experience he'd had that week in witnessing an individual offering service to a stranger.

His story was as follows:

"It is July, and in the heat of the summer here in D.C. with the accompanying humidity, it is almost unbearable to go outside, as we all know. As I was stopped at an intersection by a red light, I noticed the line of cars to the right of me, also at the intersection, did not move as the light turned red for me and green for them. I wondered why they had not moved, especially since there was a very long lineup of cars at that moment.

"I then noticed that the woman in the front of the lineup of cars seemed to be struggling to get the car to turn over. She obviously was having car issues, had a car full of young children, and from the look of distress on her face, she needed help. I expected the man in the car behind her to jump out and come to her rescue, but instead of offering help, he honked!

"This man's willingness to honk must have instigated the need for others to join in with frustrating honks of their own. I could not believe what I was witnessing. But as quickly as the honks began, I also saw another car, back further in the line, pull off the road.

"I saw a man in a dark suit jump out of the car and run to the rescue. This man alone pushed the young mother's car to the side of the road as the rest of the cars moved on their way to their desired destinations, and the man in the suit continued to attend to the needs of the young mother."

I will always remember the story this man shared and how I felt for this young mother and her humiliation and frustration. But how he ended the story left me in tears of gratitude and respect for the man in the suit who came to the rescue.

He finished, "The man in the suit who came to this young mother's rescue was our own dear friend, Brother Gary Farnes."

I sat there astonished. My father had never told us of this experience! He would never have sought the limelight or attention for his good deeds. Had it not been for this man sharing what happened with the whole church, I would have never known. I often wonder how many people have received help and assistance from my parents throughout the years without me or anyone ever knowing.

Serving in our homes, schools, community, and churches and seeking to live a life of contribution over achievement will bring about happiness unlike any other. Helping our children contribute to life in many ways is helping them with life skills, wherein they will find the success they ultimately want to achieve.

These simple principles of Prayer, Scripture study, Family Night, and Service, as mentioned above, are simple yet sacred. From experience, I can promise not only fulfillment in life but joy in the journey. These tools and principles will help you awaken the Divine within you.

Recently, as an adult, I was able to sit in a small room where gold medalist and hall of fame athlete Peter Vidmar spoke of the incredible journey that led him to multiple Olympic Medals and victories in the sport of gymnastics. His presentation was incredible and had me, my wife, and our two teenage daughters on the edge of our seats as we learned about repetition and consistency from one who lived in such a way.

After his presentation was over, a man stood and asked, "Peter, you have achieved incredible things in life, and you have been known as a Gold Medal Gymnast. Now that those days have come and gone and you are no longer competing, who are you? What will people know you as?"

The entire audience held its breath. I thought, *what an incredible question for someone who truly has been known for his athletic ability and accomplishment.* But his response was even more incredible.

Peter Vidmar took a breath and replied, "To my grandchildren, I am Poppi. To my children, I am their father. To my wife, I am her husband. But most importantly, I am a child of God." He then added, "The greatest things I am . . . are *off* the stage."

To my children and to the reader, I want you to know that you are sons and daughters of God. You are children of a God who is almighty, who is endless, who knows all, sees all, and is all. Build your foundation upon Him, and you will build to conquer.

PHASE 1 CONQUER CHALLENGE

Conquer More by making a spiritual and physical commitment to yourself and to God that your foundation will be firm, immovable, and unchangeable. Choose one thing that you will always do every day that will build this foundation. In the space below, write your foundational goals:

SPIRITUAL FOUNDATION GOAL:

(example: I will start my day with five minutes of prayer/meditation, at least five days a week)

____

____

____

____

____

PHYSICAL FOUNDATION GOAL:

(example: I will run three times a week for 30-45 minutes per run)

____

____

____

____

____

PHASE 2

BUILT FOR STRENGTH & ENDURANCE

"When thou art converted, strengthen thy brethren."

—LUKE 22:32 (KJV)

In this phase of my physical training for my marathon, my coach (Jacob Puzey) focused on the need to build strength and that this is a process that takes time to develop. Thus, with anything that takes time, patience, consistency, and trusting the process is extremely important. He said to start with the core and add resistance as needed once I had more form down.

As far as endurance goes, when it came to training me to become a runner, his goal was to train me to be a lifelong runner. He not only looked at the race ahead of me but prepared me for life. Gaining the strength at the core that I needed to withstand the resistance that surely would come, resistance that would build additional strength and endurance align so well with life.

After building a foundation, strengthening the core and my ability to endure life's challenges and opportunities was critical. During those teenage years leading up to my time to spread my wings as a young adult, I continued to be blessed in my home and by many leaders who strengthened my core, helped me develop several types of strength, and led me to the start of adulthood and the marathon of life that would surely follow.

It was in these strengthening and developing times that I learned what I would love to do in life, even if I had to do it for free. My religious mission as an eighteen-year-old young man built strength and endurance upon the foundation my life had been built upon, and not only did I do it for free, but I paid to be there. The return on this investment is priceless. Many of you reading are not familiar with what a mission in my church looks like, so hopefully, this next chapter will help you understand a little better what that entails. Here we go . . .

FIRST COMES THE LOVE

Eighteen years old, just graduated from high school, leaving my family for two years to set off on a journey that would change my life forever, a journey I had waited my entire eighteen years on earth for. In my younger years, my parents helped me build a foundation upon gospel principles. In our church, it is expected that young men serve a mission as part of their priesthood service. I had a firm foundation and some spiritual and physical strength I could rely on, but the mission was an opportunity to further build strength and endurance for life. It took strength of mind, body, and spirit to muster the courage to leave home for two years, but I also loved the gospel message I had been taught in my youth and saw this mission as an opportunity to share what I felt was a gift I had been blessed with in life.

The decision to serve a mission for my God was one I felt I made as far back as I could remember, and the time of my mission had now come. Going on a mission is one of the highlights in the life of any young man or woman of my faith. Without knowing where you will be assigned and having no ability to influence that decision, trusting wholeheartedly in God to send you where he needs you most, the day of your mission assignment arrives by way of a letter from our church headquarters. Surrounded by those I loved most, I opened the letter, which contained my assigned area of service. I opened the letter and read these words:

> "Dear Elder Farnes, you are hereby called to serve as a missionary of the Church of Jesus Christ of Latter-Day Saints. You are

> assigned to labor in the Leon Guanajuato, Mexico Mission. It is anticipated that you will serve for a period of twenty-four months."

YES! I was so excited to serve in Mexico. I hadn't even considered Mexico as I pondered the many places around the world I could be assigned to serve. But I loved it; I loved the idea of learning Spanish and the opportunity to learn a new culture and to love new people. To know where I was going was exciting, but what came next was a life changer. Words that struck my heart more than anything else I read on that piece of paper: "You have been recommended as one worthy to represent the Lord as a minister of the restored gospel."

Wow, what an honor and opportunity to represent the Lord to the world, sharing a powerful gospel message every day of my life for the next two years. This was a moment I had waited for, and a decision that has had a tremendous impact on the rest of my life. How often are you recommended as one worthy to represent the Lord and at the age of eighteen? Truly, this opportunity sunk in deep as my desires to represent Him were real.

To be ready for a mission, a missionary must live their lives in harmony with the commandments and principles of the gospel of Jesus Christ. A missionary must undergo a series of interviews to ensure they understand the responsibilities of a missionary and have kept themselves clean and ready to carry such a sacred message and mission to the world.

Had you known me growing up and the homebody I was, the severe separation anxieties I suffered, you might have thought I'd never leave my parents and the comforts of my home. But then, if this was the case, you might not have known me well at all. At a very young age I gained love, testimony, and a desire to follow whatever the Lord would ask of me.

And I knew this was my duty to my God to serve Him for two years. Was I nervous? You better believe it. I was the kid who tried to have sleepovers with friends growing up, yet when the night crept in, I would fake sickness and go home—every single time. Home was where my heart was; home was a safety zone for me. I love my family, and honestly, to this day, I am grateful I always wanted and still want to go home.

A few months out of high school, I found myself standing on a curb at a bus stop in San Luis de la Paz, Mexico, with my new mission companion Elder Castro from Mexico City, whom I had just met two hours earlier. He spoke no English, and I spoke only a few sentences of Spanish. As I stood there, in a new country, a new language, new people all surrounding me, a feeling of panic set in.

How can I do this for two years?

I couldn't just fake sickness and call home now, but I wished I could. Instead, I called upon a different home, and then some words came to my mind, which I spoke to my companion in broken Spanish: "*No se mucho, tengo mucho que aprender, pero yo amo Jesucristo y por eso, estoy aquí.*"

Translated to English, I said, "I don't know much; I have a lot to learn, but I love Jesus Christ, and that is why I am here." It was during this time of my life that I learned what the scripture "perfect love casteth out all fear" (Moroni 8:16) meant. It wasn't that I had to have "perfect" love. It was the perfect love of Jesus Christ I needed to rely on, and by so doing, my fear could be cast aside.

I feared a lot prior to going on my mission. Knowing I was going to Mexico, I feared learning a new language and worried people wouldn't understand me and the message I had to share. But that fear was quickly pushed aside as I found that even if the words didn't always come freely at the beginning of my mission, the improvement was daily, and I quickly learned to speak Spanish fluently. Pushing this fear aside allowed me to knock on doors day and night, inviting complete strangers to hear a message I came a very long way to share.

One of those doors I knocked on was that of the Marquecho family in San Luis De La Paz. Their daughter, Claudia, opened the door, and while the rest of the family did not want to hear our message, she did. So, outside the house on the doorstep, we taught Claudia about Jesus Christ and our Heavenly Father's plan. I learned so much about Christ's perfect love through Claudia and the choices she made. Her family respectfully declined our invitation to hear the messages we were sharing with Claudia. They also did not want Claudia to continue learning from us. But Claudia felt something from the messages that were shared, and she desired to become a member of our church through baptism. She was a senior in high school and eighteen years of age. So, while an adult, she was still in her youth and was choosing to make a big commitment and leap of faith. We invited her family to attend her baptismal service, but on the day of the event, she arrived on her own, ready to be baptized. I was so in awe at her love for Jesus Christ and her faith. Without the support of her family and friends, she relied on the perfect, strengthening, and enduring love of the Savior to move forward with the choice and commitment she had made. The day of her baptism was a very special and happy day, and when it was all over, she walked home alone to a family who did not support her in her decisions. But she was not and will never truly be alone as she continues to trust in that perfect love.

I was caught with great excitement and emotion when four years after my mission had ended, I received a letter from Claudia. I opened the letter and read, "You may not remember me, but I hope you do. You taught me the gospel of Jesus Christ and helped me receive sacred ordinances. I am writing to let you know that I am now serving a mission for the church in Tijuana, Mexico. The gospel has changed my life, and I am so grateful to now be able to share it with others, like you did with me." Wow! I couldn't believe it. I had to know what had happened with her family; they must have now been supportive of her being out serving a mission. As we wrote back and forth a few times, I came to find out that this was not the case. She continued to live the gospel without her family's support. She continued to move forward in faith, trusting in the perfect, strengthening, and enduring love she had come to know despite not having full support from home. From Claudia, I learned that despite the challenges we face in life, and even when we may feel alone, we do have a perfect source to turn to through which all things can be overcome.

I served amongst many who did not have a lot in terms of worldly possessions, but what they did have with family and with God always seemed to be enough.

We recently read a book at MTN OPS as part of our Conquer Book Club titled *Essentialism*. I love this book for many reasons, but it helps me bring things back to one priority in life. The word priority is an interesting one, and in this book, the author, Greg McKeown, says:

> *"The word priority came into the English language in the 1400s. It was singular. It meant the very first or prior thing. It stayed singular for the next five hundred years. Only in the 1900s did we pluralize the term and start talking about priorities. Illogically, we reasoned that by changing the word, we could bend reality."*

How did we allow priority to become priorities? How can multiple things be "Most Important?" The answer is that they can't. For me, I have found ONE PRIORITY in life that, when focused on, gives me strength and the ability to Conquer More in all aspects of life. That one priority is God. He is the ultimate answer as to how I conquer. When I put God first as the only true priority in my life and am willing to let him be the most important influence, I am more capable of meeting the demands of this life. As you read, I want you to pay attention to how each of my stories and relationships can be brought back and are affected by my first priority, God. I hope that you, too, can recognize His power and influence in your life as well.

One of my brothers spoke at my farewell gathering before I left on my mission to Mexico and gave me some wise advice. He told me, "The harder you work and serve on your mission, the more beautiful your wife will be." That made me laugh. I loved the advice, and while maybe a little superstitious and not really my reason for working hard, I did remember it, and I set out to serve the Lord with all my heart, might, mind, and strength.

My desire was to work each day with a love for the Lord and those whom I was called to serve and to do it with my light still lit to the very last day. I did feel great about the service I rendered, and as I found myself on board an airplane two years later, anxious and excited to see my family, I felt a sweet assurance that my service was acceptable unto the Lord.

Only months later, I found that my brother's promise was also true. I honestly must have been the best missionary in the world, as evidenced by my receiving one of my greatest blessings from God in Jenna Wood. Just five months after we met, she became Jenna Farnes. By first loving and serving God, I feel I was blessed to love and be loved by Jenna. She truly has been a gift more valuable than life.

Jenna and I have been blessed with four amazing children. They are AWESOME! Hallie recently turned sixteen and is driving all over town now. Yes, this scares me, but she is a really good driver. Her two high school dances, which would have been her first dances, were canceled due to the pandemic. She faced an interesting high school experience. But she has an attitude that allows her to get through anything difficult in life, and I am very proud of her.

Hallie has similar anxieties that I had as a kid and is a homebody, yet also a friend who everyone wants to be around. She has faced those anxieties like a champion, and at a young age, has found an ability to be strengthened by her Savior Jesus Christ. Hallie finds strength and endurance by trusting in God's guidance through her life. When Hallie was thirteen, we were sleeping in a tent in our backyard. I thought everyone was asleep, but Hallie gently nudged me. She asked, "Are you awake?" and after I responded, she said she was feeling prompted by God to pray about something that had been on her mind, something she needed divine guidance with in her life. I told her that if she was feeling prompted to do so, she should. With that, she climbed out of her sleeping bag right then and there, knelt on the ground, and began to pray about the subject. In this moment, and in some experiences she had the following day, her prayers were answered by God. With Hallie, I feel I have a front-row seat in the life of one who leans on God as the most important influence in her life, and because of her, I am strengthened. When I think of Hallie, I think of Virtuous. She is a blessing to our family and this world and will go on to do amazing things, just as she does now.

Kenzie is our fourteen-year-old daughter and our dancer. She continues to dance at the junior high where she attends school. Kenzie has faced some difficult times as a young child with some health issues and as a young teen with many pressures that surrounded her in those years. I was so impressed with her when, a few years back, she was the only one of her friends who did not make the company team at her dance studio.

As her father, I was devastated for Kenzie. I felt brokenhearted, as I know she did too. She still made an excellent team but had to watch as her best friends gathered for their classes while she went to hers. They were under the same roof but competed on separate teams. For a young woman in her teens, this was a big deal, and comparison could have overtaken her. Instead, Kenzie took extra classes and sought additional opportunities to refine her skills that year, a lonely time for sure in the life of a teenage girl.

The next year as tryouts came around, she got the result she wanted and made the company team, proving to herself and those around her that hard work does pay off. Watching Kenzie face this mountain of faith, while many might have quit or let feelings of loneliness or defeat overtake them was inspiring to me as her father. I wondered whether I would have faced things with such resilience and determination. Her strength and persistence bolstered mine, as I have faced my own mountains of faith. When I think of Kenzie, I think Majestic. She has a natural beauty, and this majesty comes through, especially when I see her resilient attitude at this stage of life.

Beckham is our eleven-year-old son. My only son. It is very symbolic for me to have only one son, as I relate my experience of being a father to that of God and his only begotten son, Jesus Christ. Beckham is all things *boy*. He loves sports, the outdoors, pranking people, and just having fun. If you spend any time with Beckham, you will simply laugh because of his laugh. He has the ability to truly lighten the mood and bring joy into the lives of others. When I think of Beckham, I think of the word Righteous. His life, even at a young age, is one of righteousness as a young man of God.

Beckham is an incredible soccer player with a wicked left foot. Not many can bend it like Beckham from the left side of the field. He was once the fastest kid on the field and loved the ability to sprint past other players. Then, almost overnight, he was hit with a major physical growth phase where he faced severe Sever's disease in his heels and Osgood-Schlatter disease in both knees. This had a major impact on his speed and confidence. But he has stuck to it, worked with trainers, honed his skills, and is now growing out of these pains after years of suffering and is better for the growth that he has experienced through facing his own challenges. He truly has demonstrated his strength to endure challenges as a youth. I am inspired by his perseverance and desire to grow despite the pain.

Beckham soaks up knowledge and loves to research things with a hyper-focused approach. Once he gets his mind set on one thing, you better brace yourself for a full download on all that it entails. Recently, Beck was ordained to the priesthood and now has the responsibilities of a priesthood holder.

I have seen Beckham step up his game and take his priesthood responsibility seriously. Each week, Beckham dresses in a suit for Church. He loves to dress well but also sees this as an opportunity to show his greatest respect to the Lord. Beckham is a young man of God.

Savvy is our caboose, and what a fun caboose she is. We often look back on her "I found the Lord again" story, and not only does it give us a good laugh, but it also inspires us to find the Lord again and again each day of our lives. I call her Savvylicious, and when I think of her, I think of Joy. When she was born, the nurses could not believe how good she was. She literally did not cry one time in the hospital. She entered this world as calmly as could be, and she continues to be a calm, smiling daughter to this day. Her calming influence is just what I have needed to gain additional strength amidst the challenges of life.

Savvy will be baptized this year, and she is so excited. She loves her friends, playing soccer, dancing, and tumbling, and she even wants to start her own YouTube channel. She takes turns sleeping in each of the kids' rooms throughout the week because everyone wants their time with Savvy. I cannot wait to see all that she accomplishes in life.

Savvy didn't walk until she was about eighteen months old, and while some were worried she wouldn't walk, Jenna and I just loved that she crawled all over and then sat comfortably on our laps, just as content as can be. We once heard that the longer they can crawl, the better for their brain development. I think all the crawling paid off because Savvy truly is savvy.

In the scriptures, I have many heroes. One such hero was described as having spoken to his children in this way:

> "And he did exhort them with all the feeling of a tender parent, that they would hearken to his words, that perhaps the Lord would be merciful to them" - 1 Nephi 8:37.

My feelings as a parent and as a father for my children are very tender. I may exhort them more than they would like, but I know what has brought me true joy in life. A joy that can be eternal, one that the world will not offer. I would exhort my children to know that I write this book mainly for them, for their benefit, and that they should read my words often and through them find not only my love and feelings about them and life, but my great desires to have them as mine for eternity. My desire for them to read my words is that they know of my devotion to God and my knowledge of His reality. He is not some made-up idea to give us a sense of hope in life, but he is *real*, His plan is real; His love is real, and His desire to see you, my children, happy in life is *real*. The hope I feel in God is *real*!

To my children, my plea is to find a personal witness that He is your priority and to Let God Prevail, making Him the most important focus each day of your life. When "First comes the love," let us seek to do the will of the Lord, who when asked in Matthew 22 (KJV), "Master, which is the great commandment in the law?" he replied, "Thou shalt love the Lord thy God with all thy heart, and with all thy soul, and with all thy mind. This is the first and great commandment."

To me, this is the first and greatest love that, when found, felt, and committed to, will lead to blessings in this life and in the eternities to come.

PHASE 2 CONQUER CHALLENGE

Conquer More by considering your priorities in life. Are the most important things receiving your most important attention? To truly build strength and endurance, you need to be true to the core. "For where your treasure (priority) is, there will your heart be also" (Matthew 6:21KJV):

PHASE 3
BUILT FOR SPEED

"When I was a child, I spake as a child, I understood as a child, I thought as a child: but when I became a man, I put away childish things."

—1 CORINTHIANS 13:11(KJV)

"Trevor, when you're an adult, you're going to be like a ship launched on a trackless ocean." As a teenager, right before my mission, I had to raise my eyebrows at these words. They came to me during a blessing from a church leader, and he shared even more wisdom with me before I left.

To achieve success, I would need both a compass and a destination. The destination would ultimately be returning home to the God who created me, loved me, and knew what I was capable of in this life and in the life to come. My compass would be that of following those promptings of the Spirit, which would come through obedience to the commandments of God, along with daily scripture study and prayer.

The path of discipleship was already important to me, but after receiving this advice, it gained more meaning. That destination, along with the compass, became a constant part of me and the lens through which I would view the world and my future.

As soon as I returned home from my mission, I quickly learned that the words of that man were true. I was a different person. I had grown into a man, and childish things were now in my past, although my friends and family will tell you I still engendered a childlike sense of play. Life started to come at me fast, and many decisions needed to be made that would have a great impact on my future, especially on the family I desired.

As I was training for my marathon, I thought about this period of my life—where I had been in training for some time to create an amazing future, to uplevel my training by using the momentum I'd already created in life with a feeling of speed that began to propel me forward every day. Now, in my marathon training, the more I ran, the faster I became—and the faster I wanted to be!

When running a race—even the race of life—it's important to understand the difference between speed and stamina. I enjoyed tracking my speed, but on advice from my training coach, what became *more* important to me was my ability to *maintain* a decent speed over a long period of time. What did that mean? Stamina was the name of the game. A lot of athletes have conquered a four-minute mile but can't maintain it, especially not for marathon requirements. My focus needed to be not just speed but stamina.

Stamina over speed became a consistent requirement in my training for the Moab Marathon. When I continued to think about it, stamina mattered a whole lot more *in life* as well. Life is a marathon, I realized, not a sprint. Let us build for speed that is long-lasting. This is *how I conquer* and how you can, too.

FIRST COMES LOVE (PART TWO) . . .

I was the first of my friends to leave on my mission at the age of eighteen, so when I returned home, I found myself friendless and struggled to find a new routine. I got a job working in the warehouse at my brother's company while living at home with Mom and Dad. When not working, I picked up the guitar, which I barely knew how to play. I learned songs—almost always love songs—to hopefully play for someone special one day. I even wrote a few tunes of my own.

Looking back, I feel bad for my parents and younger brother! I was not a good guitar player, but I had nothing else to do and wanted to learn. Fortunately, they were patient with me and let me play into the late hours of the night, my lonely heart yearning for the perfect companion.

After a few weeks of nonstop "musicianship," I decided I should look at getting into school. My mom and sister took me to Utah Valley University, which was fifty miles south of our family home. I got classes scheduled and started looking for an apartment closer to campus. Right about the time I should have signed a contract for the apartment, I started to get inexplicable cold feet and a prompting told me to stay up north. That voice in my heart said it would be better to keep working for my brother—which meant I would continue to *tocar la guitarra* (play the guitar) into the night.

The prompting to **stay** was strong, and it was real. When it came down to seeing the college campus and picking up that pen to put my name on the apartment lease, I had such an unsettled feeling. What I had learned growing up and on my mission was that a feeling of the spirit indicating the correctness of your decision would *not* include confusion, fear, or doubt.

On the other hand, the prospect of continuing to work for my brother felt more reassuring, and I *trusted* that feeling. Having just returned from serving a mission, loving and teaching people the gospel of Jesus Christ, I had become very familiar with those promptings and how to respond to them. It certainly was not that it was just second nature to me because those feelings don't always come that strong, but it was a voice I recognized and knew to obey.

That might have been the most important prompt of my entire life.

Learning to listen to those nudges, those promptings you receive to act—or at times, not to act—are so important to learn. It's a skill that all of us can gain, but it takes time, patience, and persistent effort. It also takes keeping ourselves undistracted by all the noise the world is offering. I learned that sometimes you just have to be still.

As a young kid, my mom used to always have us sing when a train was coming:

"Stop, Look, and Listen. Stop, Look, and Listen. Choo choo... the big train is coming down the tracks."

Crazy as it may seem, there is so much to learn from that song. For one thing, listening can give us a warning and keep us safe from trauma or pain. For another, there are so many "big train opportunities" that we could miss out on in life if we do not learn to Stop, Look, and Listen to all that we might feel inspired to do or not do in life.

One of my favorite words found in scripture is ***hearken***. Hearken means to listen and obey—*not* to hear and delay.

I heard one of my brothers once say, "To hear is different than to listen." Then, he went on to give me an example. "Let's say you are in a restaurant with your spouse or a friend. You are in conversation, yet you can hear things going on around you. You might even hear a conversation at a table next to you, the hustle and bustle of the waiters, or even the crash of a plate as it breaks on the floor. You may even be in conversation with the person you are eating with, but have your phone out, scrolling through social media or your email account while that person is talking."

It's true. All of those are examples of *hearing*. Sounds pretty surface level, nothing deep, and nothing to act upon, right? To *listen,* on the other hand, is to give your entire focus to the one speaking to you, and it doesn't happen only with your ears. **Sure, you listen with your ears, but also your heart, your mind, and your soul.** Your listening evokes a response, a call to action, a desire to progress and go deeper with that relationship. When listening occurs, roots are deepened, understanding takes place, and you are able to respond. You Connect and Conquer.

What I've found in my life is that hearkening, along with faith, has played an important role in the decisions I have made. I have not always known what the result of my decisions would be—nor even the rightness of the decision until after following the promptings. But upon taking action, the Lord has always blessed me with a reassurance of the rightness of that move or even sometimes a sudden realization of the wrongness as well. What I've come to learn is that often, the answers don't come until we demonstrate an ability or willingness to *act*.

So, following this prompting to stay at home, I kept working at my brother's office and warehouse. Lo and behold, a new gal came into the office one morning. I don't know if it was her good looks or what, but she got the job—and man was *I* happy. I don't even know where to begin when it comes to the beauty I saw then and still see today in Jenna.

Her outer appearance was stunning, a bit exotic with her dark hair and olive skin, yet there was something familiar about her, almost as if I had seen her before. She was young, fit, and confident, yet she was also kind. Her voice was unique, and that uniqueness intrigued me. Right away, I was floored by both her outward and inner beauty.

If you've ever met a returned missionary who hasn't spoken much English in a few years, you'll know what I mean when I say their English is subpar, meaning ridiculously inept. Probably the most entertaining thing is to witness one of these returned missionaries trying to pick up a beautiful girl. Probably one of the *least* entertaining things is to be one of them trying hard to impress said girl.

I remember it like it was yesterday. She walked into the breakroom where I sat at the table, probably eating Panda Express. I was wearing my yellow Abercrombie jacket that said, "Jeans Pool Service." My face went bright red, and I thought, *what do I ask? What should I say?*

The first thing that came out from my horribly broken English was, "So, are you studying?" She looked at me confused, so I repeated, "Are you studying?"

"Right now . . . ?" she asked quizzically, looking around at the office.

I was suddenly paralyzed with fear and heat flushed my cheeks. *Did I ask that correctly?* You see, in Spanish, if you were inquiring about someone going to school or were a student, you'd say "*Estas estudiando?*" or "Are you studying?"

Jenna just gave me a blank look and responded that she was just going to eat lunch, not study.

Dang, what a great first impression I made.

When I soon found out that Jenna was not on the market, it was like a punch to the gut . . . but that did not stop me from pursuing her. I learned to be persistent in my mission and that good things come not only to those who wait but also to those who go after their desires. I couldn't just sit back and patiently suffer through not getting to know her. Luckily for me, Jenna and I worked side by side in the warehouse every day. A few weeks later, I decided to approach her again.

"You know," I began as casually as I could, "one of the guys here in the warehouse wants to ask you out but knows you are currently taken. Will that keep you from going out with someone else?"

Her face turned red, and she replied, "I think so."

Not wanting to make her feel more uncomfortable than she already was, I just said, "No worries, I'll let him know. Although you need to know, he will be disappointed." I gave her a smile and got back to work.

Later that night, Jenna's dad, who was a friend of my brother's, called my brother and said, "Jenna is pretty sure Trevor was talking about himself. Tell him to be patient; Jenna would love to figure out a way to get out on a date with him."

After my initial embarrassment, I was beyond excited and could barely contain it, but did my best to stay "cool" around her. Within a couple of weeks, Jenna approached me in the warehouse while we shipped out packages and said, "I can't go out on a date, but I am going to start going to a gospel institute class every Tuesday night at the University of Utah." She paused, catching my gaze pointedly. Her eyes danced, and she smiled shyly. "You are more than welcome to come with me."

Score! This was perfect. A little spiritual strengthening with a beautiful young woman? Nothing sounded better. I told her that would be great and I'd pick her up.

Tuesday night came, and although it was "not a date," I picked her up, opened the car door, and enjoyed the class with her. I even kept those notes from that first class. I remember the beanie and jacket she wore, the cold breeze of that fall day, and the warmth I felt in her presence.

I was starting to understand why I stayed up north and didn't go to school. If I sped forward, pedal to the metal, without stopping to listen to that prompting, I'd be on an entirely different life path. But knowing that stamina over speed, being able to slow down with open ears and heart, was sometimes the better choice. It kept me right where I was meant to be with this amazing girl.

Each time we left the Institute, I would say, "I'm feeling pretty hungry and need to get some dinner on the way home. I know this isn't a date, but I'd be happy to buy you something as well." This went on for about a month and a half.

We fell in love over Chili's molten lava cake on Tuesday nights after learning the gospel and definitely "NOT ON A DATE!" I loved it!

Finally, Jenna let me know we could have an official date. YEEHAWWW! I went all out because that was the only way I knew how to do it. My parents had taught me how to treat women in my life, and I also needed her to be impressed. More than anything, I wanted her to know I really cared. I took her to an awesome Japanese restaurant, followed by a horse-drawn carriage ride. Everything was romantic, except the smell of those horses! But on that ride, I asked Jenna what some of her goals were in life. Her responses were music to my ears, and I knew I was falling more deeply in love.

We even went Latin dancing that night. I didn't know how uneasy that made her feel, but she was such a great sport. I always loved dancing, and she jumped right in. We danced the night away. From that night on, we were inseparable. I had found my best friend, the one who stole my heart—and I did not want it back.

The first time I walked into the room to meet Jenna's family, I said, "Good night." Since we'd just been introduced moments before, they all looked at me and asked, "Are you leaving already?"

I was confused but quickly found that what I had said sounded like a goodbye phrase, but in Spanish when you see someone in the evening you say "*buenas noches*" (good night). My English was still rusty, but this gave us all much to laugh about.

The worst linguistic mishap during our courtship happened when I was at Jenna's house one evening. My brother Trent had just had surgery on his shoulder and was in recovery. Jenna's father asked how Trent was doing, to which I replied, "He is doing pretty well. He showed me his circumcision last night, and it was pretty big, but he should heal just fine."

Both Rick's and Jenna's eyes widened, and I knew I had said something wrong, but I didn't know what.

Rick clarified, "His incision?" and I nodded.

But what did I actually say? I was too embarrassed to ask but could tell something was off; the two of them were doing everything they could to hold back laughter. Jenna quickly pulled me aside to let me know what I really had said. Oh man, was I embarrassed! The word scar in Spanish is *cicatriz*, which sounds more like "circumcision" than "scar." Unfortunately, there are plenty more of those stories where that came from.

The speed of our love and desire to be together was increasing by the day. Jenna was the companion my heart longed for. You might be wondering if I stopped playing the guitar and the answer is no. Did I get better? The answer is also no. But now there was a face to the words I sang, and her name was Jenna.

THEN COMES MARRIAGE

Two months later, I found myself sitting with my now father-in-law, asking for Jenna's hand in marriage. Thankfully he gave me his blessing, even though Jenna was just eighteen, a recent high school graduate. I am grateful he understood that when something is right, it is right. One thing he said as I left his home that day has stayed with me ever since. After having given young Jenna a blessing, a church leader told her parents, "This young woman can have anything she wants in life." As I drove away from the house, I thought, *if she can have anything in life, why me?*

I would soon discover why a church leader would make such a statement. Some of the reasons are too personal and sacred to share, but one thing is sure: Jenna is pure; she is kind, and she has divine qualities that allow her this kind of relationship and connection with God, the giver of all good gifts in life. I'm grateful I would get to be in the passenger seat alongside her for this amazing ride.

What truly caused me to fall in love with Jenna then, and even more so now over the years, is her loyalty to God. For me, first comes the love of the Lord, and that couldn't just be in my life. I knew if I could find someone who first loved the Lord and then me, we would be all right. Someone who loves the Lord is loyal, does good, is happy, and is kind. Not only did I want that for my own life but also the life we would create for a family.

On New Year's Eve 2002, I told Jenna we needed to go say goodbye to a friend of mine who was also leaving on his mission. Upon arriving at his family's cabin up in Sundance, Utah, we entered a candle lit, rose petal covered room.

Jenna gasped. "We shouldn't be here!" she cried, as she literally thought we were interrupting someone else's special night. Then, when I just gave her a knowing smile, she quickly realized what was going on. My friends had picked up some chicken parmigiana, and we served it as if I had prepared it (sorry, Olive Garden). I was so nervous I could barely eat, but I tried to play it cool.

After finishing up the dinner, the guitar came out, and I played an original song written for Jenna titled "Shining for Me."

Tonight, the stars are shining,
Shining like diamonds in the sky,
And now the brightest star,
Is shining for me.
Wish I may and wish I might,
Have this wish I wish tonight

I know the words sound a bit generic, but I loved the chords I strummed for this song and truly felt like my wishes were coming true.

I had prepared a pre-wedding video we watched together, which included photos of our childhood, our dating (a whopping two months), and then I read her "Cinderella" and had her open a box where she found her very own glass slippers. I knelt down on one knee to put them on her, and you know it . . . a perfect fit.

One of the slippers had a star hanging from it with the words "make a wish" engraved upon the face, so I asked her to close her eyes and make the wish; upon opening her eyes, there I was, with the ring box opened before her.

My heart leaped with joy. *SHE SAID YESSS!* The girl who could have anything she wanted in life said yes to me!

The date was set, and plans were made. A month before our wedding day, one night Jenna and I sat down together to plan out our finances. We were both aware that we would start our marriage with very little and had been taught by our parents to live within our means, so we thought it would be a good idea to figure out our finances together. We wrote it all down on the back page of an old notebook, a notebook we still have and cherish to this day.

We totaled our income, and then began to include our expenses. We both looked at each other and knew what came first before everything else: tithing and God. We both had committed at an early age in life to be obedient to the law of the tithe as taught in the Bible and with that committed, 10 percent of all our income would be paid to God. This one decision of making the Lord first in our life has made all the difference, and I truly mean that from the depths of my soul. I'll repeat: *This has made all the difference.* As for me and my house, we shall serve the Lord.

We were both so young, with very little income—just a lot of love, faith, and desire to progress. Together, we've found that this simple recipe, at times, is all you need to conquer in life (Love+Faith+Desire = Conquer). I have seen so many people focus on trying to make sure everything is perfect or until they are somehow prepared to then move on to the greatest things in life.

Sometimes, we overcomplicate how to achieve success, and so often, we falsely define success. Instead, I know it's better to just jump in and experience those great things in life. If today is all you have, don't take too long preparing that you miss out on what you were preparing for the whole time. Meredith Willson has a beautiful quote, "You pile up enough tomorrows, and you'll find you've collected a lot of empty yesterdays."

The feelings surrounding both Jenna and me writing in that notebook come back as if it were yesterday. There have been many diverse ways in which the Lord has opened the windows of Heaven to have blessings poured out upon us, and I know He has done and is doing the same for each of you who so willingly commit to putting Him first in your life.

These were wonderful times in our journey with the amazing emotions of love, adventure, excitement, and surety of what I knew I needed to be doing in life. The foundation of it all was that I knew I needed her by my side. We are coming up on twenty years of marriage and, to this day, I am so thankful for the prompting to stay and work and not go to school. I will always be grateful for having obeyed that still small voice so that we could enjoy two decades of life and love together . . . and an eternity to go. In the meantime, we've had other lessons in speed and stamina!

THEN COMES THE BABY IN THE BABY CARRIAGE!

Our first year of marriage was not our best. As a very young couple, Jenna and I had to help raise each other and mature together. I think our stubborn sides shined through in that first year, with both of us coming from similar yet different backgrounds, different traditions, and varying likes and dislikes.

I regret to say that we both displayed selfish behaviors as we tried to get "our way" in many instances. I came from a large family, and Jenna's family was much smaller. With larger numbers on my side, there were more family gatherings, more birthday parties, and just more of many things. I didn't want to miss out on any of those fun-filled events, but at times, they conflicted with Jenna's family gatherings.

Naturally, she also did not want to miss out on her own family gatherings and the experiences they were having together. It was probably safe to say that we looked like a couple of young children pouting, fighting, and giving every reason why we needed to do what we each thought was "more important." Ultimately, we went one way or another, but we went to most of those family events with bad attitudes, almost unable to enjoy the gatherings altogether. When we were around people, we put on our best faces, acting as if we were madly in love, only to end up arguing about being there once we arrived back home.

Through the initial struggles of trying to figure things out as newlyweds, I can easily look back and say there were two principles that truly helped us not only to grow but to consistently repair our marriage.

First and foremost, of course, it was about including the Lord, and not only in our finances. Just before getting married, our bishop gave us wise marital advice that has stuck with me ever since (even if I was a little slow on the uptake). I am thankful to Bishop Dave Thomas for his wise counsel; as he said, in your marriage, you get to "Look and Overlook."

He then went on to say that we need to **look for the good and overlook the bad** in our relationship. As I began to obey this counsel, I could see so much more good in Jenna than any bad could ever overshadow! In fact, when I looked for the good, which was easily found, I began to forget about any of the negatives I had previously focused on. Jenna and I had a lot of differences, that was for sure, but after marrying her, the beautiful quality in her loving the Lord I found was deep and true—it was not a courtship swindle. Amidst the struggles to figure each other out, we could turn to the Lord together and find true and lasting love . . . because of Him.

My dear friend and mentor, Clark Caldwell, often quotes Robert D. Hales, with the sage advice that couples should always focus on three simple phrases:

> "I love you; I'm sorry; please forgive me."

If we as human beings could focus on extending this type of love, contrition, and forgiveness to each other, can you imagine the turmoil we could avoid?

A therapist in Hawaii realized the power of his thoughts when it came to how he was observing his own patients. He utilized the healing power of a similar Hawaiian phrase called *Ho'oponopono*, and by using it, he healed an entire ward of mentally ill inmates. That Hawaiian therapist was Dr. Ihaleakala Hew Len, and he realized that as humans, we often create our own reality in our thoughts. To be 100 percent responsible for our own lives, we need to change our perception of ourselves—which changes the world and creates miracles.

This four-step process is what *Ho'oponopono* literally means:

"I love you; I am sorry; please forgive me; thank you."

By focusing on this process with the inmates instead of his own feelings, attitudes, behaviors, and judgments of them, his patients got better. Equally incredible, after four years, that mental ward was closed.

The second principle that helped and healed us as a couple was putting something/someone in the middle of us to focus on besides ourselves, and that came in the form of a child.

We first learned this vital lesson when we discovered we were pregnant with our daughter Hallie. When Jenna shared the news with me that she was pregnant, I could not control my excitement. In fact, my parents were on vacation in St. George, Utah, and we decided to jump in the car, drive to their vacation home, and with balloons in hand, we surprised them with the most exciting news we ever had to share.

I was going to be a dad, and I was so excited to share this with the world! While each of our children have brought an additional and increased capacity to love and feel love, Hallie came just at the right time and truly became the focus of our relationship. Jenna and I were working together to love and raise this gift from God. Hallie was a miracle to our marriage, and I consider each of our children to be miracles to life and to our marriage each and every day.

I remember that first night in the hospital when Hallie was born. Jenna was a rockstar, and I could not be more grateful for the sacrifice she made to bring this child into our lives. We didn't let Hallie out of our sight; everywhere the nurses took her, we went, and we took turns holding her throughout that first night, not wanting to put her down, only wanting her to know and feel our love.

As a new father, I was terrified for this tiny human being I helped create. Every little cough or sign of discomfort and I would push the nurse's button. I just kept thinking to myself, *how will she survive in my care?* Fortunately for our children, they have a mother who has done brilliantly at keeping them alive, safe, and cared for in so many ways.

Four children later, I can hardly stand how fast time is speeding by. It has been so important for me to remind myself that this time with our family is a full-on marathon, not a sprint. Stamina was the key, not speed. I remembered hearing older couples always say, "They'll be grown and gone before you know it." I never thought that could or would be the case, yet while they are still under my roof, I can feel time slipping through my fingertips.

So, what do we do about that? If you are a parent and wish that time could pause for just a moment for you to take it all in, I know your feelings.

As a tender-hearted parent, I long for the days my now teenage and young adult daughters would greet me at the door as children, literally singing to me as I came home from work each day. As soon as my foot was in the door, I heard, "I'm so glad when daddy comes home, glad as I can be; clap my hands and shout for joy, then climb upon his knee, put my arms around his neck, hug him tight like this, pat his cheeks, then give him what? A great big kiss!" – Anonymous. All they wanted was time with me and I with them.

I have not always parented the right way; in fact, I am always reminding myself and my children that today is the first time I have ever done *today!* I remind them and apologize to them that I am new at many things each day. The one thing I feel like I have done right is that I have given them time and attention. What is the thing I want most in my life? It is time with the ones I love most, so what do I focus on giving most in life? Attention to the ones I love.

There was a Father's Day video created by my church. The words from this video found below represent so well my feelings as a father and husband, and how this great responsibility aligns me with God and His desires as a Father to us all.

- I'm awake.
- I remember Him.
- I gaze upon them before I part.
- They lie in their bed, unaware of me watching.
- I leave.

- They sleep.
- The small home I help provide is their world.
- They play.
- They explore. Learning to move, to feel, to see, to know. Not once thinking of how it all came to be.
- Crayons, toys, books. It's all for them.
- The fridge opens, the pantry exposed.
- They expect food to be there.
- Not a thought. Not a doubt. Just hunger.
- Cereal, milk, yogurt, messy fingers, messy face. All fed.
- Tummies are full.
- Now it's nap time.
- My wife likes nap time.
- Once again they lie in the comfort we provide. All while I work.
- I'm far but close, always thinking of them.
- My phone rings.
- I only hear breathing.
- I smile.
- My wife's phone is now missing.
- I do it all for them.
- I work that they may grow.
- They trust so deeply.
- How I yearn to do the same.
- They see so little of how it all came to be. Never questioning, only trusting. I come home to second hugs.

- Now I'm a horse.
- We eat dinner, brush teeth.
- Jammie time.
- Finally it's bedtime.
- Once again, they lay their heads on the pillows we provide.
- I will be their protector.
- I will be their gentle friend.
- I will be my wife's faithful husband.
- I am a father.
- I am also a son.
- And while I may not understand all that He does for me, I do know that all that I am and all that I have is because He's a father to me.
- I now stand very aware of how it all came to be."

 https://www.churchofjesuschrist.org/media/video/2013-01-0002-earthly-father-heavenly-father?lang=eng

Of all the roles outside of being a disciple of Jesus Christ, the role of father and husband takes special meaning in my heart and soul. James E. Faust once stated, "Noble Fatherhood gives us a glimpse of the divine," and I truly believe that. Just as in the poem above that touched me so profoundly, my greatest desire is to awaken within my children the divine gifts and qualities that God has blessed them with in this life and to help them recognize the giver of those gifts and all gifts . . . their Father in Heaven.

If tomorrow was my last day, the thing I would want most for my children to always know is that they have a Father in Heaven who is always there for them, always willing to comfort them, always wanting the best for them, and it is His desire that they return home to live with Him. There could be nothing greater than this for them, not just to know, but to understand and follow.

TIME & ATTENTION

I found myself standing on a large stage in front of a sea of faces, many of whom I recognized and many I did not. Time seemed to slow. As I scanned the audience, I held a great intention in my heart to find those faces most familiar and loved by me—my family.

Finally, I found them, stage right, looking as if they, too, were waiting patiently for my gaze to meet theirs. As our eyes made contact, I saw my wife and my children's hands go up, as if to beg me not to look away.

But why? What was the meaning of their eager expression—and why were their hands raised?

Then, as I removed my gaze from my family, I slowly began to understand the experience I found myself having, an experience we all find ourselves in. I saw other individuals, groups, business colleagues, church associates, children's coaches . . . the list goes on and on, all raising their hands as if to bid for my attention.

As I looked around, I found, to my amazement, that the stage I was on and the scene before me was that of an auction. . ., and I was the auctioneer.

Again, I scanned the crowd, and again, the hands waved in my direction. They were bidding for my time and for my attention. I cared about each person and desperately wanted to connect with each one whose hand rose, yet I knew I could not. Some hands were raised, and I knew I had given and should continue to give time and attention in that direction. As I gazed out upon the crowd, again my eyes rested on my wife, my children, and those I held most dear. They again eagerly raised their hands with an expression of anxiousness.

It was right about this time that my alarm clock went off, and I slid out of bed onto my knees as was my daily custom to start with prayer. Generally, I used this time to recognize God and ask for a blessing upon the day. As I knelt this day, the vision continued to play before my eyes, and I couldn't believe that the dream seemed to continue on, even though I was now awake.

Whose bids did I accept, and whose did I reject? Who did I disappoint? It was clear to me now that I was auctioning off my time and attention, the most valuable gift I could give.

What do I most desire in life?

It is time with the ones I love most.

As a child, I grew up in a family where love was measured by time. My parents did the most amazing job of teaching us the kind of time we want with each other. The time they talked of, rejoiced of, preached of, and, in a way, prophesied of was eternal.

You see, my mom set out, obviously including my dad, on a mission to create a "family why" or mission statement and did so by naming all the kids in my family, seven of us in total, with the first letter starting with T. There is Tim, Trisha, Tyler, Tami, Tara, Trevor, and Trent. Try saying that real quick. No, seriously, do it! As kids, we would time ourselves, and so would our friends, to see who could say it the fastest. I still have friends who, when I see them, will repeat the names as quickly as they can.

But seriously, what do our names have to do with time? Our collective initials are T.F, which represents "TOGETHER FOREVER," our family motto. What awesome parents we have, who teach us that this would be the ultimate blessing for a family: to have an eternity being Together Forever?

You are probably wondering if my parents' names start with T? Nope, they're *Gary* and *Mary*! Go figure.

So, this morning, as I was still experiencing the stage and hands going up every second, the clock was ticking, and I had to make decisions. Some time went to my God, time to my family, time to my work, friends, new adventures, time to mourn, time to rest, time for every season.

Long after the dream and vision, I had to ponder: *How do we value our time? Are the lowest bidders receiving the lion's share?*

Just a few days after this experience, I was unexpectedly sitting in a hospital room with my wife and her family as our Grandma Ne slipped peacefully from this life to the adventure that is yet to come for all of us. The day before her passing, she came in and out of consciousness. Every time she opened her eyes, they were sparkling. Every time she opened her mouth, profound truths came forth.

She spoke of her excitement to move on. She said, "Love those close to you, forgive those unkind to you, and appreciate every day you have to live. Time is so precious; use it wisely."

She challenged us to stay close to each other. She wanted to make sure she didn't leave anyone unpaid. I was struck by how honest and sincere she was.

My mind raced back to the stage, and I set forth to seek out those things that would bring the greatest return in my life. More importantly, I sought out those whom I could lift, knowing that therein true happiness could be found. A quote I love and try to live by was spoken by a friend and mentor of mine named Kevin Hall: "They rise highest who lift as they go."

Who in that audience could I lift?

Building a foundation, whether it be spiritual, physical, mental, or social, requires our time and attention. We can be so easily distracted by the many hands reaching up, eager to pull us their way. Laying the foundation as early as possible and helping our children and others do the same will allow for greater strength to not just survive, but to thrive.

As I shared with you before, at MTN OPS we have an incredible "why" statement. I have my own "why" statement which is: "To awaken the divine within all those God blesses me to know." I will remind you that God himself has the *greatest* mission statement of them all, which is: "For behold, this is my work and my glory—to bring to pass the immortality and eternal life of man" (Moses 1:39). In simple words, He wants us to return home to live with Him.

There was once a time when Jenna and I were sitting with our three oldest children. Hallie had to be around ten years old, Kenzie was eight, and Beckham was about five. We were sitting in the family room around the ottoman, trying to keep their attention as we shared a gospel message.

I was talking to them about the love God has for them as their Heavenly Father and that my greatest desire in life is to teach them to know and feel my love as their father, but even more so the love from their Heavenly Father. I asked them if they knew what it felt like to feel God's love.

Each of the kids said something like "warm, good, happy." All these answers were right, and as we discussed further, a *very* distinct impression came over me to kneel with them in prayer and to pray in that exact moment for them to know and feel God's love for them. So, we knelt down and had what I felt to be one of the more sacred experiences of my life.

As I spoke the words of the prayer, I felt as though my words were not my own. It was as if I heard the very tone of my voice change to a softer, kinder, deeper, and more understanding voice. I prayed to God the Father, asking Him to help my children feel and know in that moment what it felt like to feel His love. Life stood still; silence engulfed the room, and then the warmest feelings of love encircled us.

There is a scripture that states, "I have beheld His glory, and I am encircled about eternally in the arms of His love" (2 Nephi 1:15). This feeling of being encircled about eternally and beholding His glory was exactly what we were feeling. I almost wanted to open my eyes during the prayer to see what Heavenly being we might behold.

When the prayer was finished, our eyes opened, and even Hallie said, "Dad, your voice changed during that prayer." Oh, how I wish my voice would sound that kind, warm, deep, and discerning at all times! But for a moment, the love and will of an earthly father was combined with the love and will of a Heavenly Father to let these children know how our combined, encircling, and eternal love for them felt.

As my children read this, Hallie, Kenzie, Beckham, and Savvy, each of *you* are the greatest reasons for living. May you always know and feel the combined love both your earthly and Heavenly Father have for you. You were made to conquer, and it is through Him and His love that this is possible.

I would challenge you to find ways to conquer through connection and relationships. As I have sat in various meetings, whether it be in church, work, or in the community, and especially during the pandemic, I was reminded again and again how important it is to connect with one another.

Youth especially are struggling right now because they are more connected to people through devices with no real "face time." Relationships provide us with a way to connect and conquer. Connect with friends who bring out the divine within you. Most importantly, connect with God who *is* all that is divine within you. For me, connection with my wife added a new dimension to life that has been one of the greatest connections and blessings of them all.

PHASE 3 CONQUER CHALLENGE

What is a relationship in your life that deserves more stamina than speed? What is one action you can take right now that will enable you to create stamina for the long haul and deepen that connection for the next six months? How will you make them a priority with your time and attention?

PHASE 4

BUILT TO CONQUER THE MOUNTAINS

"The mountains shall bring peace to the people, and the little hills, by righteousness."

—PSALM 72:3

Mental toughness is key to facing the physical challenges of a race . . . and life. During my marathon training, I quickly found that running hills was incredibly important to my success. The main reason why was because I didn't want to run them; hills are hard. My mental approach to them wasn't very positive—who wants to climb a giant mountain when you're already struggling on the flat road?

But here's what my mentors taught me: doing and then conquering the things you don't want to do will make you stronger, increase your confidence, and build the mental strength that will get you to the end of the race. It also translates powerfully to the unexpected mountains of life that we are often faced with. We cannot go around; we have to build up our ability to get up and over.

Running steep hills and harsh mountains naturally increases your physical strength. The significant increase in resistance can build incredible muscle strength in your quads, glutes, hamstrings, and calves, and it can do it in a shorter amount of time. I have discovered that oftentimes, in life, it's the mountain-like challenges we face that will teach us things much quicker than just about anything else. So, it goes with building both kinds of strength.

They say that running hills can reduce boredom when your goal is to power through a high number of miles in your day. I find this a bit funny because of that added strain, but in a way, it's very accurate. Nothing can shake things up in your routine and add variety quite like a good mountain or challenging obstacle showing up in your way.

I chose to run a marathon that would take me into the mountains. Some might think I'm an idiot, but there was a method to my madness. Not only do I love the scenery and creations that are so present for us to enjoy in majestic southern Utah, but I also love what the mountains of life can represent. I did not train to run a marathon because it would be easy. I intentionally chose to run a marathon—and more importantly, a very difficult marathon—because I wanted a challenge. I wanted to see what I was capable of and more. I love to *liken* my experiences in life to an eternal perspective, to challenge myself to see a bigger picture for learning. I found it a great exercise (pun intended) to learn through my training, and specifically, by facing the mountains in front of me.

Are there any mountains you're currently facing in life? Or are there some hills you often avoid because you just don't want to deal with climbing them? Sometimes, we're all faced with mountains that are unavoidable. I'd like to share one experience with you that showcases how my family and I were dropped right in front of a seemingly insurmountable cliff—and what we did to finally reach the summit.

A STORM OF FINANCIAL DIFFICULTY

"And there arose a great storm of wind, and the waves beat into the ship, so that it was now full."

—Mark 4:37

In 2006, Jenna and I were blessed with an opportunity to build our first house on a half-acre property located on a beautiful country road surrounded by stunning farm fields. I could hardly believe we were in a position to make this a reality! I was only twenty-six years old, and Jenna was twenty-four. We sold the condo we were living in, and our little family of three moved in with her parents to save some money while our new home was being built. Hallie, our firstborn, was just three years old.

At the time, I was still working for my brothers selling pharmaceuticals, and things were really starting to pick up for us. In the last two years, I worked my way up to sales account manager. Our team was crushing it, and I had created a great, six-figure commission, which kept growing. I felt confident in our ability to build the home we both desired at such a young age, allowing space for us to have more kids and create new adventures. Everything seemed to be going better than I could have imagined or planned for.

On what seemed to be an ordinary night, I kissed my wife and fell fast asleep in our bed. No sooner did I close my eyes than I heard what seemed like a voice coming from the distance. Staring into the blackness, I strained my eyes as it got louder, and I listened more intently. The words I heard were these:

"There is a storm of financial difficulty upon the horizon."

That chilling message hit me like a ton of bricks. I sat straight up in bed. Glancing at the clock, I realized I had been asleep for a while, and it was the middle of the night. I wanted to wake Jenna to ask if she had heard what I heard. But she looked to be sound asleep, and so I laid back down and closed my eyes.

An unknown amount of time later, the words came again:

"There is a storm of financial difficulty upon the horizon."

Again, I shot up in bed, this time in a great sweat. I was hearing and feeling what felt to me like a very powerful and loving voice; whether in my dreams or right there in the room, I could not distinguish the difference. At that point, I felt and knew I was being given an extraordinary message from God.

Before laying back down, a passage of scripture came to my mind. It was one I had read many times in my life, which now rang truer and more relevant to me than ever before. 3 Nephi reads: "And it was not a harsh voice, neither was it a loud voice; nevertheless, and notwithstanding it being a small voice it did pierce them that did hear to the center, insomuch that there was no part of their frame that it did not cause to quake; yea, it did pierce them to the very soul and did cause their hearts to burn."

Those were the feelings that voice provoked, piercing my very soul in a way that truly did cause my heart to burn—and my mind to wonder.

Exhausted, I laid my head back down to sleep. Yet again, for a third time, the voice returned. The same simple yet powerful warning echoed in my head and sounded in my ears.

"There is a storm of financial difficulty upon the horizon."

Once more, I found myself sitting up in bed. This time, I looked around with the desire to see the origin of this voice. I sat there for a while now, in another sweat and deep thought and wonder, not knowing what to do with this personal and heavenly message. I couldn't wait to tell Jenna in the morning. After the third time, I just lay there, unable to fall asleep.

When morning came, excitement filled me, but I also felt anxiousness begin to set in as I contemplated our financial situation and plans. Could that message actually come true? Everything seemed to be going so well. As soon as Jenna woke, I shared the experience with her, and we both wondered what needed to be done and learned from this experience. She, too, was excited and a bit anxious about what had transpired.

When I got into work, I asked my boss, who just happened to be my brother Tyler, if everything was good at the company. Was my position secure? Did I have anything to worry about? He reassured me that all was well, and things were better than ever.

So, with that reassurance, my wife and I continued with our plans, but we did it all with a sense and desire to protect what financial resources we had accumulated. We put a little extra away in savings, built a food storage in our new home in case of a rainy day, and first and foremost, to show our devotion to God, always paid our tithing first and tried as often as possible to make a generous offering to help the poor and the needy.

We had now been settled into our new home for a short period of time. Everything seemed to be falling into place: We had been married for over three years; we were enjoying our first daughter, Hallie, who we absolutely adored, and Jenna was now pregnant with our second beautiful daughter, Kenzie, who was born just months after moving into the home. While always remembering the words of my dream and the feelings that pierced my heart, it started to feel more and more like a distant experience and not relevant to our current situation.

ARE YOU A BUFFALO OR A COW?

When a storm approaches, will you respond like a buffalo or a cow? Well, what's the difference, you may be wondering?

When a storm approaches, a cow's nature is to turn away from the storm and begin to run from it. You'll see whole herds engage in this behavior. The problem is that the storm eventually catches up, and the cow often runs with the storm for a prolonged period. The elements can take a toll on the cows, who continue to try and run from the storm yet end up often weaker from the struggle. Some even die.

The buffalo, on the other hand, when seeing the approaching storm, will turn and face it head-on, running into the eye of the storm, exerting its effort to pass through the storm much quicker than the cow. The buffalo is strengthened because it chooses not to run from the storm but to pass through stronger by facing it head-on.

In the early spring of 2007, my little family and I began to face a series of difficult events, and now we were facing the truly harsh reality that the storm we had been warned of had arrived.

SICKNESS

In March 2007, Jenna and I were out on a date celebrating our fourth wedding anniversary. My mother and father were at our home with the girls as we enjoyed our time together when the phone rang. It was my mom. She was worried about two-month-old Kenzie. She wasn't acting right, had a high fever, and kept making a faint grunting noise that had her concerned.

Jenna and I quickly ran home to find our baby restless, noticeably tired, and uncomfortable. We gave her some Tylenol and hoped she would sleep well and get better. By morning, we knew something was not right, and Jenna took her to the doctor as I went in to work.

Not even thirty minutes into my workday, I received a call from Jenna with the doctor on the line. Her words sent a chill through me: "I can either have an ambulance quickly take her to Primary Children's Hospital, or the two of you can take her there ASAP, but she needs additional medical attention immediately!"

I didn't understand what she was saying, but there wasn't time to question. I raced home, and Jenna and I broke every speed limit as we made our way to Utah's Primary Children's Hospital. The ER doctors, knowing we were on our way, quickly took our lifeless baby in their arms, laid her on a table, and multiple nurses and doctors worked on her feverishly for what felt like an eternity. Jenna and I clung to each other. We were clueless as to what was happening, and our tears fell in our helplessness that the doctors didn't seem to have any answers. All we knew was that her white blood cell counts were through the roof, which told us she was fighting off something, but what?

My father and Jenna's father arrived at the hospital to help me give my daughter a priesthood blessing. I held Kenzie in my arms as my father and father-in-law also placed hands upon her head, and by the authority of the priesthood, which I held and as her father, I uttered words I had never said before. They did not feel like my words at all but from a power greater than me: "I command you to be made whole."

Can I do that? Is that power truly available to me? A confirming power and warmth pierced my soul as I felt a strengthening reassurance from God that this was *His* blessing to His daughter, Kenzie. I was simply the conduit to facilitate this powerful healing experience for my daughter, who was so loved by her Father in Heaven that it made me tremble. For a small moment, it felt as though Heaven and Earth combined, and the love of both earthly and Heavenly Father united in an extraordinary way to bless an extraordinary, little child.

A couple of hours later, Jenna and I were still sitting in a room of constant medical visitors. A doctor came in and said, "We think we will be able to save her."

"What?" we cried. Then we calmed. We hadn't known exactly how serious it had been—that she had actually been on the brink of death, but the reaffirming peace from the blessing of her to be made whole allowed us to stay calm through this storm. We sat in quiet confidence, knowing that God was on our side. Even still, the ongoing pokes, prods, needles, tests, and bouts of our sweet baby whimpering left us uneasy and anxious for answers.

About three hours in, Kenzie's white blood cells were still dangerously on the rise, and the doctors said they would need to do a spinal tap to check for spinal meningitis. I tried hard to be strong as they asked me to hold my Kenzie's little legs up to her head, bending her back to allow a small space in her spine to stick a very large needle to retrieve spinal fluid for the tests.

I had seen that needle before. It was the same needle used for an epidural during labor and delivery for an *adult*. A needle my wife Jenna won't let me talk about or describe, but it was horrific to see it injected into my poor two-month-old's frail and tiny body. Worse, no numbing was done, as they said it would be quicker, less painful, and easier on Kenzie. The pop of the needle into Kenzie's spine was audible; screams of anguish from my little Kenzie as I held her were unbearable. I wanted to scoop her up, allow that blessing of healing to take effect, and escape all this discomfort.

Suddenly I noticed blood coming to the surface of many of the pores on Kenzie's head. It was at first even more horrifying, but I was immediately struck with a reminder and a sense of profound peace and gratitude as I thought of the words of a scripture, Doctrine and Covenants 19:18, and the sacrifice, burden, discomfort, and anguish my Savior Jesus Christ felt: "Which suffering caused myself, even God, the greatest of all, to tremble because of pain, and to bleed at every pore, and to suffer both body and spirit"

I was shocked with a feeling of how God must have felt in anguish as he watched His son. *How could he have watched this suffering of His son?* I realized this mountain I was facing, one of the most profound moments of my life, could help me understand God. It was undeniably profound in every way.

Kenzie was hospitalized for about a week, with hundreds of family members, friends, coworkers, and neighbors praying on her behalf. It was a good thing because what brought Kenzie into the hospital was an E. Coli infection that went into life-threatening sepsis.

Through this, they found a urinary issue that required her to take medicine that caused her to vomit every day. A mishap with insurance that would take me ten pages to explain here caused us to have to put her on her very own insurance plan. She was deemed uninsurable, which soon would become a very difficult financial issue for our family to solve. We got over one mountain—her emergency—just to face a marathon of others, as this was just the beginning of our financial struggles.

IT ALL BEGAN TO CRUMBLE

It was as if the moment I wrote that check, a trigger would be pulled that caused everything around us to crumble financially.

Three months after Kenzie's hospitalization, in July of 2007, Jenna and I were excited to try our wings and start our own business, as this was a dream we'd been working on for some time. I had been working with my brothers for several years now selling pharmaceuticals. Since we had a great amount of savings put away, we felt ready to live our dreams as an entrepreneurial couple.

Two opportunities piqued my interest. One was in real estate, as it was flying high, and the other a retail opportunity. Yes, (sigh) it turned out that 2007 was not the best time to start into real estate . . . or many kinds of businesses. I bought two properties with my brothers. One was a large property with an old home, beautiful view, and lots of potential. We tore the home down and began to develop the property only to find issues with the county and an inability to subdivide. We had overpaid for the property in this case, misled by the agent. We sat on this property for a bit before selling it at a loss.

The other property was a single-family home on a short sale. The family was going to lose the property to the bank. I met with the husband, struck a deal with him and the bank, and signed a contract for him to rent the home back from me after the purchase. It felt like such a great opportunity. I had an asset that would appreciate, with equity and a renter who would create some cashflow for us.

Four months in, all seemed great until one night while on vacation, I got a call at 1:30 in the morning. The voice on the other side of the phone was that of a frantic woman, "Is this Trevor Farnes?" When I responded affirmatively, she went on, "The Trevor Farnes who owns my home? *You* own *my* home!" she cried out. I now knew who it was, but I had no idea that she did not know her husband had sold their home. She had been unaware of all their financial difficulty, and as she sobbed, I couldn't imagine the pain she was facing and the distrust she must have felt for her husband. We spent hours in which I was able to calm her nerves and establish some trust, but it was too late for their relationship. They divorced, and their world, which already seemed to be crumbling, shattered. I felt so horrible for them—so horrible, in fact, that when he stopped making payments on the home, I gave him the grace to catch up.

By November of that year, we had gone far too long without payment to make this a deal we could hold on to. Fortunately, we were able to sell the home, putting an end to my first go-round with real estate.

The second opportunity that my wife and I invested a lot of time and money into was within a retail franchise. After a period of due diligence and research, we decided to invest in this venture.

I won't disclose the name of the retail opportunity as it is not my intention to point the finger or reflect negatively on anyone. We all make mistakes, and we all have equal opportunities to repent and make amends. My hope and prayer is that many lessons have been learned and hearts healed by all those involved.

In July and August of 2007, my wife and I personally guaranteed multiple leases on retail locations with high traffic volume down in Las Vegas, Nevada. The contracts cost tens of thousands of dollars for the business we were running, inventory was purchased for each location, and employees were hired, many of them moving from Utah to Vegas, including my brother.

Finally, after a three-month delay and more lost funds, we were able to open the doors, and traffic slowly began to trickle in. We weren't willing to participate in certain iffy business tactics to ensure high commissions, so the traffic we did receive did not yield the same financial results we were expecting. Jenna and I were beginning to find that what had been presented to us with this opportunity was maybe not all as it seemed.

More issues arose with our stores in Vegas. At the beginning of 2008, we found that much of what had been presented to us for this business deal was not as it seemed, and our ability to run anything properly halted. Zero revenue could be collected, and we sat waiting for a miracle to occur. In the meantime, many of our good employees who were friends moved on to more secure opportunities. I did not blame them. As their replacements were hired, I had multiple employees steal money from the stores and dealt with a few break-ins. I just couldn't stop the fuse from getting to the end. It felt as though everything was about to explode.

So that spring we decided to close the Vegas stores' doors and open just one location in Utah where I could control more of the outcome. However, closing the stores did not end our financial troubles in Vegas. My wife and I were still on the hook for multiple five-year personal lease guarantees. Nobody seemed to want to forgive any debt, contract, or even work amicably to ease the burden.

We were stuck. Liens were placed on our home, and threatening letters from vicious attorneys seemed to find their way to our mailbox every day. Collection agents showed up on a regular basis at our home, and we were served legal documents at our doorsteps more times than I'd like to count.

IT'S ALL GONE

The storm of financial difficulty continued for many years, and we held on as tightly as we could. One Friday morning, in 2009, however, everything changed. As I sat working in my home office, I heard Jenna coming down the hall. The door flew open, and with tears streaming down her face, my wife collapsed to the floor. I could not help her get her emotions under control, no matter how many times I asked what was wrong.

All I could hear her say through her sobs was, "It's all gone . . ."

"What is all gone?" I kept asking.

Finally, she replied, "I just got into our bank account, and there is nothing there, Trevor! It is all gone."

I suddenly collapsed in disbelief next to her on the floor. *What? How could this be?* Our account had been slowly draining, as things were not going well, but there was still a substantial amount of money for us to get by on. But as I logged on to our bank account, I was struck with the harsh reality that what my wife said was true.

It was all gone.

OUR LAST HOPE

Our last hope to make it with this retail business came down to this one last store in Bountiful, Utah, where we ran on faith, hope, and credit cards. My wife had started selling jeans on the side to help support some of our daily necessities. As it would go, we ended up selling more jeans out of our bountiful location than the intended product of that store. It seemed to me that we were not meant to make it in this business. I went to job interviews and was offered jobs, only to sit in the parking lot wondering what I was doing. Had I given up on my dreams? My wife would just look at me and tell me she knew what we should do and what I wanted to do, and a job would just distract from that. So, more credit cards, more faith, and more hope. This retail business was not for me, but neither was a new job. While the business was not for me, I always knew there was a reason we got involved in it in the first place. Many of the reasons were for the growth of me and my wife, growth that prepared us for other business opportunities, leadership abilities, and most importantly, a greater faith and connection with my Savior Jesus Christ, all things we will continue to discuss in this book. Some of the reasons were found in some of the connections and relationships we made along the way. As I look back on these experiences, I see there were many reasons for us going through all that we did, too many for me to share, and some I'll share later in this book. There were two people my path crossed that come to mind as I think about why I needed to go down this path of financial struggle and ruin, two people for whom I would do it again.

"I KNOW WHO HE IS"

The first individual upon my path was not directly involved in this business. This individual will more than likely never remember this experience, nor will they ever know what could have happened or the terrible pain that could have come about had it not been for this business.

When building out our Bountiful store, I did it myself with only the help of my brother and brother-in-law. I am not much of a handyman, so it took longer than normal, but I was fresh out of money to do it any other way. We used all the fixtures from our Las Vegas stores to furnish our new location. I was working fourteen-to-sixteen-hour days to get this store open to the public and get revenue coming in. I would almost always arrive home around nine or ten at night.

One night, during the summer of 2008, I felt completely wiped out, depressed, and about to give up. The mountain in front of me simply seemed like something I would never be able to climb. I got ready to head home when a sudden burst of energy engulfed my body, and I had an impression "TO STAY" longer. I thanked God for the additional strength, and knowing my kids were already asleep, I felt as though I should follow the prompting and use the newly found energy. The more work I could get done, the closer to an opening, which we desperately needed.

I stayed at the store until 1:30 am working feverishly to finish that night's project. Where did that energy come from? I was running on strength from above.

At 1:30 a.m., I left the store with a twenty-minute drive home. I exited the freeway and made my way onto an old country road. The road had several residences along the way, but not many, and they were fairly spaced out with big yards. I only had just over a mile left to get to my turn. Right around the corner I would reach the comfort of my home ready to collapse into my bed.

Suddenly, a car speeded past me. I couldn't believe the speed at which they were driving. I was in a thirty-mile-per-hour zone, but it seemed as though that car was going at least eighty. It caught me off guard, to say the least. Only a few seconds after the speeding car passed, I saw something up in front of me in the middle of the road.

I thought for sure whatever it was had been hit by the speeding car. I did not want to come upon something that had been hit. I saw it move a little, but the street was dark, and my only thought was that it was a dog. The thought of coming upon something that was suffering was disturbing to me. I saw it move some more, and as I slowed down and got closer, it seemed to be moving slowly in the same direction I was going, in the middle of the road. But it was not a dog.

Could it really be . . .? I thought in shock. I couldn't believe what I was seeing. It was a young child, walking down the middle of this country road in his pajamas. I immediately pulled over and ran to the child, scooped him up, and brought him to the side of the road. He just stood and looked at me. He couldn't have been a day over two years old.

All I could think was, *how did that speeding car not hit this child? Why on Earth is he walking down this street all alone at almost two a.m.?* Our neighborhood was small, with most people knowing each other. I was close to home and did not recognize this child.

My first reasoning was that maybe he was the grandchild of the people who lived in the home he was in front of. So, I took this child by the hand, reassured him that we would find his parents, and we walked to the front door. As I knocked the lights flew on in the house and a nice older lady with white curlers came to the door in her robe.

I asked, "Do you know this child?"

She did not and could not believe that I had found him out on that dangerous country road. With all the cars that used this area as a speedway, especially at night, she could not believe he had been walking safely down the middle of the road.

My next step was to call 911. We had a neighborhood directory put together for our church congregation that I provided to the police, and they used that list to do a reverse 911, calling out to all the surrounding households to have parents check for their children.

Can you imagine getting a call in the middle of the night from the police asking, "Do you have children in your home? Are they in their beds?" Many frantic parents rushed to their children's rooms to find them sleeping soundly.

By that time, we had woken a few neighbors who were now on the scene, ready to help this child find his home. It was the craziest feeling because all of us knew each other, yet none of us knew that boy. Everyone took a picture of him and started door to door, waking up the neighborhood to explain the situation.

"Do you know this boy?" everyone asked. As I knocked on the doors, more and more people funneled out of their homes in pajamas and robes to assist in the search.

It had now been over an hour since I found him. I stood there on the curb, and with a prayer in my heart, I asked God to help us. The boy didn't talk much, didn't know his last name or where he lived, and was very much afraid. He was facing a challenge that no kid should have to deal with. As I stood on a curb with this child by my side, my prayer to God was this:

> *Father, help us find this child's family. Nobody knows who he is or where he lives. Please help us.*

As I prayed, a sweet reassurance came to my mind from God: *"I know who he is, and he is the reason why you stayed late tonight."*

This boy was the reason I was prompted to stay at our store, working late with some added energy from above! A thought came into my mind to travel with the cop back up north. Suddenly, a certain family came up. I wasn't sure if they were in the directory, but maybe this little boy could be a relative of theirs.

I asked the cop if we could drive that way since it was not a short walk, especially for a two-year-old. As we drove, a call came over the radio. The boy's parents had called, and it was the house I had thought of.

As we pulled up, they stood on the side of the road, desperately waiting to hold their child. Expressions of thanks that they felt could never be enough were shared. A family sleepover, in the backyard, on the trampoline was where this little boy's journey began as everyone silently slept. This was their relative's house, which was why nobody knew the boy's face. While we did not know, God knew this boy.

God knew me, and God strengthened me to stay a little longer to work a little harder, not necessarily for my personal benefit but definitely for the benefit of this young boy. How many of God's children are walking dark and lonely paths? Maybe you, as the reader, are walking a dark and lonely path at this moment. Maybe you are a parent whose child is walking the dark and lonely path that life can sometimes offer, and your prayer is that someone might find them, scoop them up, and help them find their way safely home. Are we willing to stay, let God strengthen us, and then follow the promptings He gives us to rescue his wandering children? Sometimes the mountains we face as we go about life can only be conquered as a team. We need many willing hands to come out of theie comfort zones, even in the darkest nights to help us push forward and to get over the last ridge before we reach the summit or that journeys end.

Again, I think back on the story I shared of Christ as he was with the people who had waited so long to see his face and hear his words. Let us all remember that "HE STAYED." There will be moments when our presence and a listening ear are needed by another. Will we *stay* and listen? When the gentle nudge tells us to stay a little longer, will we muster up the courage to do so? When God speaks, do we listen?

On that quiet drive home that night from my store in Bountiful, Utah, the Lord was able to use me as an instrument in His hands for the benefit of another. It is totally fine that this boy may never even remember what happened to him that night. To me, what was most important besides him being safe was that I hearkened to God's gentle nudge, his gentle command, and his gentle voice TO STAY.

WOULD I DO IT ALL AGAIN?

The second individual God needed me to meet through this journey of heartache was a man named Greg. The outcome of our relationship and the improvement of both of our lives by knowing each other is that first, I would struggle financially all over again. Our little low-rent store was our last chance to keep this retail business alive, and we quickly began to realize it just was not going to work. There was no cash left for the business, and the credit card bills were creeping up quickly. We now did not have enough runway to take flight with this opportunity. It could be a good opportunity for someone else, and maybe we just needed to build the foundation for them, were my thoughts. So I listed it for sale.

There wasn't much of a business to sell, so I listed it for just the price of the assets within the store, the price of which would mean a great deal for my family. I received a call soon after posting the listing. The voice on the other end was friendly; the man's name was Greg, and he asked if he could come visit the store. The next day, the man who entered the store was not as I expected, and shame on me for judging a book by its cover, but I quickly thought, *this is not the person I want to sell my store to.*

Greg's appearance was a little rough around the edges. He had long hair, a long beard, earrings, many tattoos, and even a few gold chains around the neck, with a few around the wrist as well. Greg didn't come across as the sharp businessman who could make this succeed.

If things don't go well for him, is he the type of individual to come after me financially or even physically? What I quickly found beyond this rough exterior was a man with a heart of gold, with a hope and desire to provide for his family with this business opportunity. Greg made an offer, and I accepted.

I required half down and the other half within six months. As part of the deal, I promised to take Greg to a sales and marketing training in California. As I packed my bags for the trip, I felt a gentle nudge through the spirit to pack an extra copy of the Book of Mormon.

Since my mission, I had continued to listen to nudgings and respect them. I also was nervous because I knew that many people on the planet had huge misunderstandings of my faith—which happens amongst a lot of religions. One of the biggest was how many didn't know we are Christians. Part had to do with our nickname of "Mormons" when the church's official name is The Church of Jesus Christ of Latter-Day Saints. In fact, I held in my hand another witness of Jesus Christ that confirmed and complimented the truths of the Bible, which I regularly read and believe. So, when I felt prompted to grab a Book of Mormon before my trip, I listened.

Well, we flew to California, had a great few days of training, and then it was time to fly home. We sat in the airport waiting to board a delayed flight, and a young man sitting in front of me asked if Salt Lake City was my home. I told him it was and asked about his home as well. He said he was going to visit Salt Lake City for the first time.

"So, what do you recommend I do in Salt Lake?" he asked.

"Have you heard of Temple Square?" I replied. It was springtime, so I knew he'd probably like seeing the beautiful temple grounds with the variety of flowers and trees in all their blossoming colors.

He had but wasn't sure if it was going to make his to-do list for this trip.

I started to explain that if he wanted to truly understand some of the history of our great state, he should spend at least a few hours at Temple Square.

Then the young man asked, "Have you served one of those missions that lots of Mormons do?"

That was my opportunity to share the Book of Mormon I had in my bag. I told him about my two-year experience serving in Mexico and what a great and life-changing experience it was.

As I spoke, Greg, who had been sitting behind me, facing away from me during that conversation, quickly sat up in his chair. He turned around and came to sit by me.

"I served a mission, too," Greg began.

I stared at him in shock.

"In Louisiana," Greg continued with a grin. "And it was the greatest two years of my life! I got to serve people and teach them of Jesus Christ every day."

What! Wow, had I truly judged a book by its cover? Greg went on to share how important the mission he served was and even shared some feelings he had about the Book of Mormon itself. It was at this point, right before boarding, feeling tingles up and down my arms and a warmth within my soul, that I pulled my extra copy out and gave it as a gift to this young man. I never heard from that young man again, but I hoped, and continue to hope that he has enjoyed that blue book that has meant so much to me in my life.

Greg and I did not sit next to each other on the plane, so I was not able to speak to him about the experience we both had. We caught up at baggage claim. While walking to my car at the airport parking lot that night. Greg said, "You know, that was kind of fun sharing about my mission."

"Man, I had no idea that you served a mission, or that you were inclined religiously at all!"

He then told me that it had been over twenty years since he had stepped foot in a church. I found that there were many reasons for this, and that his faith and belief in God had dwindled significantly. I quickly came to realize that the gentle nudge I felt by the Spirit to take that book with me on the plane served two purposes... Yes, I hoped it was a blessing to the young man I gave it to, but almost more important in my heart was the sudden excitement Greg found in remembering his mission, his experiences, and a spark I witnessed in this man's eyes that night as a result.

I spent two more weeks with Greg, training him at the store. Much of our conversations ended up around God, faith, and family. I challenged Greg to read the words of Christ with me each day and we did. Over time, I invited Greg to come to church with me and my wife, and he accepted. As he began to show up to things that were once important to him, he began to see their importance once more in his life. Greg eventually was even called to ecclesiastical leadership roles in his own local congregation, something he felt would never be part of his life again.

In our church, a pinnacle moment for its members is that of going to one of our sacred temples to receive special ordinances and blessings. One of the highlights of my life was when Greg and his wife asked Jenna and me to go through the temple with them for the first time in over twenty-five years. For Greg, being back within the walls of that sacred building was something that took time and effort to accomplish. It took lifestyle changes that were not easily made overnight. But because I listened to the promptings in my heart and offered a hand, that was a mountain my friend didn't have to climb alone. He reached the summit, knowing that faith didn't have to be lost forever.

We all have mountains to climb, and faith is a huge part of that journey and reaching our own individual summits. Your journey may never look like mine, Greg's, or your friends'. It's meant to be uniquely yours. This is truly the way to Conquer More in life. How can you choose to be a little better today than you were yesterday? And a little better tomorrow than you were today?

THE BEST INVESTMENT WE EVER MADE

Waking up to nothing in our bank account, truly seeing that it was all gone was a harsh reality I never thought we'd face. For a young couple, we had saved up quite a bit of money, but it had quickly disappeared. What had happened? Right away, after doing my best to console my wife, I began to investigate.

Well, the financial institution who held our checking and savings accounts was also the bank where we had set up a business credit card. Honestly, without knowing it, I had a $300 minimum payment on the business card that had gone past due. The bank, instead of taking $300 out of my account to make that minimum payment, took every cent we had out of our personal account to pay off much of the balance on the card. It was no small amount, and it was gone. All of it.

I'm telling you we had $0 to our name.

Have you ever found yourself in that situation?

This situation can either be the worst or the best situation you find yourself in, depending on how you look at things. Yes, I was anxious and angry at the bank. I made multiple attempts to get them to reverse that and take two months of minimum payments. In fact, I begged them, to which they replied, "There's nothing we can do."

So now what were we to do? Well, Jenna and I found ourselves on our knees again praying, pouring our souls out to God for help. I called my father that Friday afternoon, who, in his kindness and wisdom, brought us a fifty-dollar bill so that we had enough to make sure our children were fed for the weekend and assured us that we would figure out a game plan come the following Monday.

Jenna and I did just that. We went to the store and bought some milk and bread. We now had forty-three dollars to our name. On Saturday, I looked at Jenna and said, "I think I know what we need to do with that $43." She replied that she did, too. In our church, we have what is called a "Fast Offering." Beyond a tithe, there is a donation that you can make as part of your fasting.

Once a month, we fast for twenty-four hours, and the money we would have spent on the meals we skipped can be donated to help those in need. Jenna and I decided to start a fast that Saturday afternoon, and we would pay our $43 to the Lord as an offering for those in need. I had always been taught from the scriptures, but also from my parents and leaders, that when you put God first, all things will be added unto you.

Handing that $43 over to the Lord to help those in need was the most freeing feeling I've ever had in my life. We had literally given our all, all that we possessed when it came to financial means, and all our hearts to God in prayer.

As I was on my knees, I truly felt that more than ever before, I had 100 percent turned my life over to Him. To my amazement, I found I was at 100 percent complete peace because of it. I looked at Jenna. She was equally serene, and we just hugged each other.

As a couple, we faced that day with complete confidence in the Lord. He gave us that strength and confidence. When you realize that you are not in control of everything in life and that God is, when you turn the controls over to Him, when you are able to let Him prevail in your life, a true sense of peace, confidence, and assurance will be yours. This was our experience, and I knew I could face the future knowing that God would prevail, direct, and support me—support us—along the way.

What happened the very next day left us in utter shock and gratitude. We received a refund check in the mail that we were not expecting. In fact, we were not even aware it was coming as something had been miscalculated on an obligation and a refund was sent to us.

As Jenna and I stared at the numbers, we couldn't believe what we saw. It was almost the exact amount of money that the bank had taken from us for the credit card. Once more, we fell to our knees and recognized the Giver of all these gifts. It was incredible.

The question I would ask anyone suffering is: How much are you willing to *give*? How much are you willing to *trust*? How much *faith* do you have to step into the unknown? I am here to tell you that the more you give to God and to His children, the more you trust in God and His will, and the more you are willing to step forward in faith, the more you will succeed!

Answers to prayer and responses to our giving have not always come that quickly. Oftentimes, we are met with what I like to call *Divine Delays.* Let those delays test your faith, patience, and trust in Him. In time, you will always come off as a conqueror. Find strength in staying a little longer, *joy* in sacrificing a little more, and confidence in the hand of the Lord.

The best investment I could ever make in life is that of trusting my all, my abilities, my efforts, and my well-being to the Lord. I challenge you to test me in this, and like the scriptures say, "See if God will not open the windows of heaven and pour out a blessing that you will not have room enough to receive" Malachi 3:10.

Soon it was the time of year I usually love so much, when people reach out to help, love and support others during the holidays. I often hear people saying, "It's great that we help others during the holidays, but we should do it all year round." I agree, but if you've ever struggled financially, you'll know that the holidays, especially when you have kids, can make financial burdens seem that much harder.

Thanksgiving was a day I was looking forward to during those struggling years because I knew we could go to our parents' houses, eat as much food as we could possibly handle and not worry about our children being hungry. Whenever we would go around the table to express what we were grateful for, without any hesitation I said, "FOOD." As a father especially struggling in those years to provide, food was always on my mind. Did my children have enough? Did they feel hungry like I did? My heart has always hurt to think about any child feeling hungry, but now mine were hungry at times, and it was a constant in my mind.

That Thanksgiving, with my spirits high, Jenna and I got the kids ready to head out the door. Literally twenty minutes before leaving for my in-laws where the feast awaited us, I heard a knock on the door.

There stood a woman with a manilla envelope in hand and a sheepish look in her eyes as she stretched forth what I knew she carried. It wasn't the first time we had been served legal documents. But on Thanksgiving Day? I stood there stunned, looked past her to the street where I saw her little family waiting for mommy in the minivan, husband in the driver's seat.

All I could say was, "Today? Really, today?"

Her response was that they were passing through the area on their way to a family dinner, and it was convenient.

Shocked into silence, I signed my name to the delivery notice. The look in her eyes and countenance told me she was already feeling the pain of her mistake on this day, so I pushed no further.

Our house was now in foreclosure and had actually just hit the internet for auction. What was a day of happiness, gathering, and feasting ended up being a day of me just being eaten up inside. It became an all-consuming struggle to figure a way out. The next day, I immediately called the bank. They told me they had no choice; the foreclosure and eviction would be coming. We fasted; we prayed, and we called everyone we could. For some odd reason during the struggle, I would find glimpses of hope and peace and a reassurance that all would be well.

For example, the kind lady with the mortgage company on the other side of the phone who reassured me that she felt our pain and was doing everything she could do to find a way for us to stay in our home. I could feel her sincerity and desire to help us, and I felt as though we could trust the work she was doing on our behalf. There are good people in this world who truly do go above and beyond in the service of others, not just seeing their job as a job but an opportunity to serve. I will always be grateful for her and others who did likewise.

These little glimpses and peaceful moments were what we hung on to. For anyone struggling with anything like this or anything in life, hold on to that hope. For me, hope came from a Savior, and it was through his strength that I was strengthened. I truly was too prideful to admit to neighbors, family, and ecclesiastical leaders how much we were struggling.

If you've ever started a business, then announced that you were open for business, only to find yourself having to close your business, you know how I felt. I had failed. Nobody would ever think highly of my ability or capability again if the world found out how badly I'd fallen.

While I felt this would be how people would perceive me, I was so grateful that I never felt this from my wife. Jenna believed in me when I felt nobody else would. My children were too young to think anything of me other than that of a superhero. I was so thankful for that. As long as I came home each day, wrestled with them on the floor, built forts with them out of pillows, and tucked them in with a kiss on the forehead and the words, "Sweet dreams, my sweet little angel," each night, they were content and blissfully unaware of the roiling fears inside of me.

Just when I thought all our efforts were spent, merely within a few days, I got a call from the bank where we had mortgaged our home. That kind lady, with her sweetest voice ever said, "Mr. Farnes, we have one option that had been rejected as of yesterday that I was able to approve today. We can modify your loan if you start making a reduced payment today."

That was the answer to our prayers. That which was once rejected was now approved!

How did we conquer what yet again felt like an insurmountable mountain? For me, it all comes back to the Lord intervening and finding a way. I have gained a special appreciation for those whom He can use as instruments to bless those so very much in need in the hours they need it most.

We now knew we would have a home for the holidays. Our children could still sleep in their beds, and we were able to do it avoiding bankruptcy. That was a Thanksgiving time of year I will never forget.

CHRISTMAS MIRACLES

A week before Christmas, I sat in my office. No gifts had been bought, and we didn't know how to make Christmas morning special for the kids. As I sat there, Jenna texted me with a picture of a bike. Beckham had asked for a bike that Christmas, but we could not afford one.

The text included a picture of the bike and the words, "Should we buy this for Beckham? Only $2". Jenna had found the bike at a local thrift store called Deseret Industries. Staring at the run-down thing, I thought, *how did we get to this point, where all we can afford is a $2 bike?* With hesitancy but no other choice, I responded with a "yes."

I'll never forget that Christmas Eve. I've never spent more time on a gift than I did with that bike. It was black and blue and all scratched up. The tires would not keep air, and I didn't know how to fix them, nor did I have money to buy the supplies to make it happen. I washed that bike with water and soap and scrubbed it as clean as I could. I pumped the tires up, and then thirty minutes later, I pumped them up again.

There was an even bigger issue: the pedals had broken off. We were giving our son a bike with no pedals! We had a little girl's bike with pink pedals, and I got the wild idea to take those pedals off the girl's bike and add them to Beckham's bike. I would use black paint to paint the pink pedals. I tried and tried for hours to get those little pink pedals off that bike to no avail. We put the little chunk of metal bike under the tree with a bow around it, and then I laid there in my bed the rest of the night, unable to sleep, heartbroken that this would be the gift my son would run out to Christmas morning.

And so, Christmas morning, my son, my only son who wanted a bike, who I wanted to give a bike to, came running out to a little black and blue bike with no air in the tires and no pedals. My heart ached that Christmas morning until I watched as he saw the little Lego sticker I had left from the previous owner on the front bar post of the bike. "A Lego bike" Beckham hollered with excitement. Beckham thought it was "the coolest thing ever!" to have a Lego bike and never did I hear him say a thing about any disappointment in the clunky, dysfunctional piece of metal gift that sat before him. It was a bike he was never really able to ride, yet he never shared any disappointment in what was received, only gratitude.

Oh, how I wish I could receive as Beckham received that day. Finding the good in a bad situation. At such a young age, he was able to keep the focus on the good and overlook the bad. No wonder we are supposed to learn from little children.

There was another Christmas a few years later we prepared for six months in advance. We had enough bad experiences waiting until the last minute while broke that when this opportunity arose, we took it. My oldest brother and his family were getting ready to go on a mission for our church. They would be moving away for three years, and as they prepared to move, they filled a large trailer full of old items to be hauled away to the local thrift store.

Truly wanting to help them in their move (but also with the additional motivation to see what was on the trailer), I offered to take the trailer to Deseret Industries for them. Did I go straight to Deseret Industries? No, with their permission, I took the trailer straight to our home while the kids were in school, and then Jenna and I sorted through everything on the trailer.

We found some true treasures and gifts that our children would love and enjoy. There were two beanbags for our oldest girls, a Batman fortress for Beckham, and lots of little dolls for Savvy. We found clothing to fit each child. We felt like we had hit the jackpot, and we truly did. We hid away all the items, and we were set for Christmas way ahead of schedule.

With the rest of the stuff, along with other belongings of our own, we put on a yard sale. Our kids had wanted to go to Disneyland for some time now, and it just was not in the cards. But, come the day of the yard sale, we raised enough money to make the drive to California and spend four days in the park. It was absolutely incredible, and we felt so blessed and grateful to my oldest brother and our inspired thriftiness. Where there is a will, there is a way, and I am so grateful for the helping hands, the leftover clothes, household items, and gifts that made that trip and the gifts for Christmas possible.

I WROTE THE CHECK

After having invested in that retail opportunity and seeing it all quickly dwindle away, I was upset for a time with the individual who sold us the stores. I struggled with having lost what we had. One night I knelt in prayer, pleading with God for strength—pleading with him for *anything* that felt like movement in the right direction.

I then voiced my frustration with that individual who I felt had done us wrong. Our financial momentum was halted and suffering, and I felt frustrated with the feeling of having to start over. I was also frustrated over my wife's frustration and worry. She didn't deserve or need this in life; I was supposed to provide.

Suddenly in that moment I was shown the truth. I was called to the carpet. The words "I wrote the check" stung me to my core. *I* had made the choice to write the check for that opportunity. Were we misled a bit? Yes. But *I* decided to write a check for multiple stores. I could have done just one, and it would have hurt much less.

That night, as I knelt, my paradigm shifted, and I stopped placing blame on outside people and forces. I started to take accountability for my choices. It also occurred to me that this was something I could learn from. In fact, I have since learned that slow, calculated, and disciplined growth is the way to ensure longevity in most things we confront in life. I wouldn't be trying to climb *that* mountain again because I knew the pitfalls I'd encounter.

After maturing and repenting, I sometimes wondered how I would feel if I ever saw that individual again. What feelings would that encounter create? Well, a few years later that opportunity came. While I was meeting a friend for lunch, I suddenly spotted him across the room at another table. After an immediate surge of emotion, I took a breath and walked over to him. I shook his hand, asked how he was doing, and continued on my way. Honestly, I was overjoyed to find that I carried no feelings of resentment or ill will. That was a big gift to me. Later, I read a quote by Malachy McCourt, who said, "Resentment is like taking poison and waiting for the other person to die." The reality hit home. I had stopped taking the poison. I did the inner work and no longer carried the negative feelings that once resided within me.

I pray this man, as well as others who find themselves in similar situations like him, can also learn from those experiences. Isn't that what this life is all about? Can we all be a little more helpful to one another in learning and growing from the many harsh realities and experiences that life can throw at us? I learned that it is possible not only to learn but to create a greater ripple of love. Where could you do that in your own life to Conquer More?

I invite you to use these challenges that everyone inevitably faces, to build your confidence: confidence in yourself, in those coaching and surrounding you, and most importantly in God, who can and will be your strength when the mountain seems insurmountable.

THE HEART OF THE MATTER

When 2010 came around, I thought hard about what I needed to do to rebuild my family's foundation. We were making our minimum payments on the mortgage and other debt, making sure we were just hungry instead of starving. But it was time to go back to the most important part of conquering: having a solid base.

So, for the next three years, despite my hesitation, I made my way through six different business ventures, some of them within multi-level marketing companies. Each one had appeals, and some worked out but only temporarily. Certain nudges led me in, and other nudges brought me out, knowing they weren't the right fit. If I kept going, I'd lose my footing and tumble down the mountain I'd already been bruised trying to climb.

With grit, or, as I call it, "stick-to-it-ness," we ventured into our seventh business. In my heart, I knew this time things would pay off. And believe it or not, it had to do with the actual human heart.

I started this next venture with the heart in mind: a heart health product we called L-Arginine Complete. Why the heart? I have a history of heart disease in my family. I wanted to create something I felt I could fully put my heart into, something that would make a difference for those I loved and others who have loved ones who could benefit.

I found some research done by Doctor Louis Ignarro, who won the Nobel prize in 1998 for his work with nitric oxide as a signaling molecule in the cardiovascular system. I bought his book and found a chemist, and together, we worked up our first formula. Our first guinea pig was my father. There was an important reason why.

My father's father died of a heart attack. My mother's father died of a stroke. My father, at the time, had some stents put in his heart to increase blood flow. He was in bad shape. The doctors didn't know why my dad had not had a heart attack yet. His left anterior descending artery (otherwise known as the "widow maker") was completely blocked, and it was only placing the stents that saved his life.

Even then, his doctor told him he would more than likely have to undergo open heart surgery within about five years. At this time, he was diagnosed as pre-diabetic, and one of the most obvious signs of his heart issues was his constant rubbing of his fingers together.

You see, he had severe cardiovascular neuropathy that he had struggled with for years, meaning he was not getting enough blood flow to his extremities, so his fingers and toes were numb, and even his toenails had stopped growing. His cardiologist at the time told my father to take 1000mg of L-Arginine each day—an amino acid found to convert to nitric oxide in the body. This nitric oxide dilates the blood vessels and arteries and allows for more blood flow, having a tremendous effect on the cardiovascular system. To my dismay, we discovered that as much as my dad desperately needed this, the 1000mg dose was not effective.

Through my research studying the work of Dr. Ignarro, I found that with a daily intake of 5000mg of L-Arginine and 1000mg of L-Citrulline, a person would gain a prolonged production of this molecule nitric oxide in their body, allowing for a longer lasting nitric oxide boost and all the benefits of increased blood flow that came with it.

With the help of a great chemist friend, we had our very first sample, and we allowed my dad to take it first. Within a few days, a tingling sensation came back into his fingers and toes. By the end of the month, his toenails were even beginning to grow! We knew we had something, but I also knew I had nothing.

I had no money. I had no way of bringing this product to market. So I visited with my brothers, who had seen major success in their business ventures. Gathering my research and my courage, I asked if they had any desire to invest in this project with me. They loved the idea of the product, the opportunity to help our own loved ones, and even the dream of preventing heart disease *in our own lives too.* They decided to take a chance on me and the product.

The company icon was a phoenix, and for many reasons this was a new life and a new start, just like the fiery phoenix rising from the ashes. I, too, needed a restart—something new. New confidence, new opportunities, and people that would be the start of my desired success.

Our site went live in October 2010. I did everything to start this new company except fund the production of the product. I worked with the chemist to create the product and the manufacturer to get us the finished goods. We ordered 350 bottles to begin with. It felt like such a large investment at that time.

And I was all in, no matter what had to be done, to ensure success. I built the website, designed labels, took customer service calls, shipped out the orders—you name it. Luckily, we had an accountant who helped us manage the small amounts of money that were coming through. I did this without a paycheck for the first five to six months. Not feeling confident enough yet to ask for additional investment, I wanted the business to produce the income I needed for my family and prove it could grow.

Life got really busy right then. It was a time when I felt like I could dare to challenge *anyone* in the world to a "busy challenge," and I would have come out on top. While working at the office one day, I spotted an ad on the internet for a bachelor's degree in internet marketing at Full Sail University. This was perfect, and I needed it, but how in the world would I pay for it?

The feelings I got when I looked into the degree program were powerful and overwhelming. I felt a strong prompting to gain this education. I felt that if I were to go to school, which I had tried many times, always dropping out for my business pursuits, this would be the degree that would be most applicable and relevant to what I was doing and wanted to continue to do for my career.

Doubtful of the outcome, I looked into their student loans and got approved. Within a month, I was a student at Full Sail University! It was all done online; in fact, I never stepped foot on the Florida campus until a few years after I got my degree. I was on a business trip and got to take photos in front of the school I was so proud to call mine.

With three little ones at home, we had our hands full, just starting a new business, no money in the bank, and now school. What else could we add to our plate?

Right about this time, while watching my brother's kids while they were on vacation, I got a call. The man on the other end of the phone said, "Trevor, this is Steven Christensen. I'm wondering if I could meet with you over at the church this Sunday."

I said that would be fine, hung up the phone, and then asked my wife, "Is Steven President Christensen's first name?"

We had to look it up and found it to be the case. In our church, our congregations are called wards, and each ward has around 300-500 people in it. In a geographical area, a set of 8-12 wards make up what we call Stakes. Steven Christensen was our Stake President at the time. *Why on Earth would he want to meet with me?* I wondered.

That Sunday, I was asked to serve as a counselor in the bishopric of our ward to a newly called Bishop, Robert Wilkes. I was honestly shocked. I was twenty-eight years old at the time, and this had always been a calling for more mature and experienced brethren, in my opinion. But without hesitation, I said yes.

In life, my main priority and goal is to always do what the Lord asks me to do, even when it doesn't make sense. God's ways are not our ways, and so while feeling very young and inadequate, I accepted.

Upon leaving the office, I honestly felt like there had been a mistake. What if Bishop Wilkes had wanted someone else, and my name was written down by accident? But I just waited until the next Sunday when the callings were announced in our congregation. Literally, until they said my name, I felt like they were going to realize there was a mistake and they would need to apologize and call someone else.

But, sure enough, my name was read from the pulpit to serve as a counselor in the bishopric. We were asked to take our new place up on the stand, sitting in front of the congregation where I would find myself every Sunday for the next six years. That seat was uncomfortable to me, but what was comforting was to look out each week at individuals who made sacrifices to serve each other, including my family. Plenty of those faces were struggling with hardship, testimonies, seeking answers to prayers, and relief from their own storms.

At the end of that first meeting, I walked out of the room and down the hall toward Sunday School. An older brother from our ward stopped me in my tracks, put both hands on my shoulders, and looked me in the eyes.

"I bet you feel young for this," he guessed.

I responded assuredly, feeling the weight of it all.

He looked even deeper into my soul and said, "'Let no man despise thy youth,'" repeating the words of Paul to Timothy in the Bible from 1 Timothy 4.

I was so touched by the love and confidence I felt from this dear brother that I pressed forward with faith, knowing that if God called me to this position, he would provide a way for me with all my inadequacies—and my busy schedule—to succeed and do as much good as possible in this position.

Not wanting my new ecclesiastical leader to know the load and schedule I was now bearing, I didn't tell him about school. I didn't want him to worry about my ability to serve in this calling. I needed the traction this calling brought to my life and the ability it would give me to forget myself, my business, my school, and just serve the times I could.

My new schedule looked a bit like this: Monday-Friday, I worked from 7a.m.-5p.m. Once the workday was over, I would put on the student hat and do homework at the office from 5p.m.-8p.m. Sometimes by 10p.m. at night, I got home, hopefully with enough time to kiss the kids goodnight, then watch a short show with my wife before being zonked out in bed.

On Tuesday and Wednesday nights, as Bishoprics, we would meet for two to three hours for church meetings, to visit the members of our congregation, and assist wherever the Lord needed us.

Saturdays from 8-5 were spent doing more school work, but Saturday evenings were now my precious family time. Then, anxious to be prepared and sharp for our Sunday meetings, I would escape around 9:30 to take a steaming hot bath, relaxing me enough to put me to sleep, then wake up at five o'clock Sunday mornings for a 6:00 a.m. meeting at the church, typically getting home between two and four in the afternoon. Not once did I do any work or school on Sunday. That day was dedicated to the Lord and to my family.

On Monday, it would start all over. I was busy. Somehow, the Lord always helped me find time to get the tasks done and, most importantly, to help my family feel loved.

After those first six months, I was finally able to start taking a small income from our business. It was just enough to pay tithing, the mortgage payment, a small amount for gas, and $300 for groceries each month. God bless my wife for stretching that $300 for groceries.

Remember the story about the warning of the Storm of Financial Difficulty Upon the Horizon? Well, we had created a great food storage for ourselves, and we had now been living off it for some time. When we created that food storage, I had felt it would be for a time of earthquake or major natural disaster. Never did I think the food storage would be used in a financial downturn that our family would face.

We cracked our own wheat from the food storage and mixed it into just about everything we made to give our meals more substance. For those not used to eating this way, which I was not, it was rough on our stomachs. Stomach aches from our food storage food were a common occurrence, but it was better than being hungry.

When I first launched our new site selling our cardiovascular formula, I thought we would be an online sensation overnight. I was wrong. The internet was a hard place to compete in when I had no marketing budget, no experience, and had gotten myself into one of the most saturated marketplaces on the internet: supplements.

After about three days of our site going live, I was laying on my couch at home late one night. I refreshed my cart analytics, and there was our first order. I couldn't believe my eyes. Not only was it our first order, but the order was for twelve bottles! *What?* I still have the picture of me shipping that first package out of our one-room HQ. In that one room, we (I) did all the customer service, shipping, marketing, social media, label design, web development—you name it.

That one room became a sacred place for me and eventually for those I was fortunate enough to add to the small team. Every morning in that small office, I knelt in prayer at my desk, begging God for miracles to occur in my life and with this business, always remembering to thank Him for those many blessings that oftentimes got overlooked through the struggle.

In that office, behind locked doors, you might have often found me in tears. Often, those tears came while on my knees, tears of a pleading, struggling young father who was willing to work in whatever way God told him to in order to make things work for his family.

I shipped that first order out to a doctor, and I followed it up with a call. First, I wanted to thank him for the order (he had no clue he was my first customer). I then asked him about why he chose our product and why he purchased the quantity he did. He responded that he needed a product like this for his patients who suffered with high blood pressure. He also said he had a lot of patients who needed increased blood flow to help with their neuropathy.

These were all things I had created this product for. They had helped my dad with these very issues, and I now found that there was an industry outside of the online marketplace that I could go after. From there, I reached out to similar doctors whom I knew, some who even knew my dad and loved his success story on the product.

I told them all that I'd give them a free bottle of the product if they would email all their colleagues about it. They started doing it, and while it was not the online overnight sensation I had hoped for, it was progress, and progress was what I desired more than anything.

Recently, we just hit the twelve-year mark for that business. Twelve years is an incredible accomplishment for any business owner. Inr my previous experience, I was lucky to have my doors open for three to six months. Now, looking back on over ten years, I am beyond grateful to God for allowing me to find something that gave me slow, steady, sustainable growth.

There were countless mountains that my family faced during this stretch of years. We've been able to rise above and beyond them together. Remember what our little daughter struggled with as a newborn? Kenzie is now sixteen years old and as healthy as can be. We are grateful for her faith and the faith of others on her behalf to be made whole and to the master healer who saw fit to bless her to recover completely.

We each are given gifts from God. To God, all things are spiritual, and if we have eyes to see, we will find those heavenly gifts. I feel that one of mine is an ability to liken experiences in life to an eternal perspective. God will demonstrate to us the grandeur of His being, His mission, and His plan if we open our hearts to His.

We, as his children, have the responsibility to look for all that can be taught, understood, and learned by simply choosing to see things with a greater and more eternal perspective, an eternal perspective that I believe God wants us to have.

PHASE 4 CONQUER CHALLENGE

Has there been a time in your life when you felt like, "It Is All Gone!" Like you are left empty? Write about that experience on the lines below, and describe how you conquered that time.

____

____

____

____

____

____

How have you found *joy* in your journey, no matter the circumstances? If you have struggled to do this, what do you commit to doing now to ensure you find *joy* in your journey?

____

____

____

____

____

____

I hope that my words and experience as you continue to read will help you find the source to fill those empty spaces.

PHASE 5
BUILT TO BREATHE

"The Spirit of God hath made me, and the breath of the Almighty hath given me life."

—JOB 33:4

Have you ever heard the lyrics by Sara Bareilles, "Head under water and they tell you to breathe easy for a while"? I remember hearing those words during our years of financial struggles and always thought to myself, *that's exactly what I feel. People encourage me and are there for me, but I feel like I'm fully submerged in my challenges. Breathing isn't easy to do. Sometimes it even feels impossible!*

There were many times when panic attacks, anxiety attacks, and everything in between, left me feeling out of breath. It was almost more than I could handle.

However, there's a difference between suffocating under our pain and having our breath taken away; the former is a pleasant, gratifying experience. And there were many times when moments of miracles, both big and small, took my breath away, knowing that the hand of God was behind each one. At that time, when I could finally take a big inhale, I felt overwhelming love and awareness of my creator.

So, what do you do when your head's under water and you don't know how to get any air? Figuratively and physically, we're going to talk about how you can breathe easily.

From a physical standpoint, as part of my marathon training, I truly had to learn to breathe differently and know that I was built to breathe in an incredible way that would produce a more able me. Rather than shallow chest breathing, I was taught to breathe deep into my belly, a technique that uses my entire lung capacity and stays within me longer and allows me to work more efficiently.

Consistency and intensity have been a theme for me in both my physical and spiritual pursuits. First, I focus on doing things consistently over time so that my body, mind, and spirit can build the strength it needs. As my body gains strength, I increase the intensity of the routine to elevate my performance. When it comes to breathing, this approach was very applicable, and the more consistent I was in my training routine, the stronger my lung capacity and breathing became. As my ability to breathe increased, my intensity began to increase. I could go longer and further than I ever had before.

I would run eighteen miles on a Friday and turn around on Saturday and run twenty more. It was an incredible feeling to breathe effectively and in a way that allowed me to endure. Learning to breathe in marathon training is of the utmost importance. Breath both controls and maximizes your performance. Breath coordination, timing, and efficiency help you reach your full potential.

Breathing is a beautiful thing. When was the last time you took in a breath and thanked God for that one simple life-saving breath?

"Life is not measured by the number of breaths you take, but by the moments that take your breath away."

—Maya Angelou

Fasting is a way I have been able to learn how to breathe as I've trained for life, pushing through some of the most difficult obstacles, scarcity, and more. Fasting is a spiritual concept that I grew up practicing... and during all the economic hardships, fasting was a way I increased my capacity to handle more stress, push past comfort zones, and breathe into the struggle—and then beyond it.

Fasting has been shown by science to have many benefits to the digestive system and managing weight, which is why intermittent fasting has become popular. It is linked to the nervous system, can calm anxieties, and raises awareness in the body.

I could say I probably fasted close to 200 times over our seven years of famine, for twenty-four hours at a time, to have something finally pay off and give a good return on the time, blood, sweat, and tears that were invested into creating a successful business. To this day, it is still not unusual for me to fast a couple times a month for the continued success of MTN OPS and all those who are involved in it.

If you are reading my book right now and have never fasted, I want to share some steps I use to make my fast most effective and intentional.

First, I try to fast for a purpose. Your purpose for fasting can vary to a large degree. But I have listed a few examples below.

1. Fasting for the health, well-being, and even healing of an individual.
2. Fasting to find strength in any of your current circumstances.
3. Fasting to be more humble or have an increased ability to forgive.
4. Fasting for help with finding a new career path or better employment.
5. Fasting for assistance with finding companionship.
6. Fasting for strength to overcome anxieties or weakness.
7. Fasting for patience with a relationship that has been stretching you.

The list could go on and on. I have even found it very fulfilling to do a fast of thanksgiving, going without food or water and then expressing gratitude throughout the day to God for all I have been given that I might sometimes overlook. These have been some of my most rewarding fasts.

Once I have a purpose for my fast, I find a quiet place to pray. I personally like to kneel to pray, but this does not need to be the case. I would, however, recommend a nice, quiet place to really think about your purpose for fasting, undistracted from the noise of the world while you pour your heart out to God.

To get down to the very basics for those who may not know how to pray, my prayers usually go something like this, in this order:

1. I address God by saying "Heavenly Father."
2. I give thanks: (I share anything with Him that I want to express gratitude for.)
3. I ask: (I then ask for whatever I am in need of. This is where you can express your purpose for fasting and ask for the blessing you seek.)
4. Express: (Express anything you wish to share with God.) He knows the thoughts and intents of your heart, but as your Father, He loves to hear from you. If you are a parent, don't you love it when your children share and express themselves to you? The great thing about God is that He is a much better listener than most of us parents, and we as His children can feel Him listening if we go to Him with real intent in our hearts.
5. I end the prayer by saying "In the name of Jesus Christ, amen."

It is that simple! My fast has now started, and I typically like to fast for twenty-four hours. This is really hard for many; I know because it is hard for me. If your health is sufficient, I would challenge you to do so, but if it needs to be shortened, that is okay. Do what you can to make the sacrifice but do what is healthiest for you. Know that sacrifice brings forth the blessings of Heaven.

Russell M. Nelson has taught, "Fasting helps your spirit develop dominance over your physical appetites. Fasting also increases your access to Heaven's help, as it intensifies your prayers."

As I go without two meals during twenty-four hour period, to make my fast more meaningful, I donate the money I would have used to buy my two meals to charity, to help those in need who might be less fortunate than I. Whenever possible, I pay a much more generous amount than the cost of two meals and have found that as I am generous with God, He has always been generous to me. Generosity to God with our donations, as well as our time and attention to those things He would have us do, is simply by far the greatest investment we could ever make. The return on this investment of time, money, and anything that He has blessed us with will far surpass any financial investment we could make in this life.

During this period of fasting, it is important to keep our hearts, minds, and souls in tune with God. Keep our thoughts heavenward and focused on that which we seek. Keeping a prayer always in our heart can be difficult amidst all that we have to do and get done daily, but the effort to keep a spiritual focus during those twenty-four hours is very important.

When the time of my fast is over, I end it the same way it began—with a prayer. I again find a quiet place, undistracted from the noise and business of life, and follow the steps I mentioned earlier. This time, however, I, let God know I am done with my fast and give Him thanks for the strength I had received to accomplish the fast. I reiterate the purpose of my fast with God and again ask for His blessing to be with me for this purpose.

I will always remember a time in 2011, during our many financial struggles, when, after driving home from church, I noticed Hallie, who was seven years old at the time, stayed in the car. I waited and watched and finally went over to the car to see what she was doing. As I peeked through the window, I saw her kneeling down in the back seat, praying. I didn't interrupt, but when she got out, I asked what she had been doing. She said, "I was finishing my fast."

I asked what she had been fasting for, not knowing she had been fasting. She said, "I was fasting so that things will go better for you, Dad". Her faith almost knocked me off my feet. Truly, a little child shall lead them. What seven-year-old decides, on their own, to intentionally go without food, turns to God, and asks a blessing upon her father? Thank you to Hallie and each of my children who, on many occasions, joined me in fasting and prayer and who also did so in the quiet of their own lives at very young ages.

It felt so good to have a company we were supporting the chiropractic industry with. A company with products that help others breathe easier and get more oxygen and blood flow to their bodies. But I needed it to get into the hands of more people more quickly. I knew it was possible, but I didn't have the team to do what I desired. My wife and I prayed earnestly about how to get our products to more individuals who could benefit from their effects.

What we didn't know was that at the same time, three individuals were running a marketing company, and they wanted something to back that changed, enhanced, and improved lives as well. They wanted something they could dedicate themselves to outside of the many contracts they had with brands that were not their own.

In early 2014, while talking to my neighbor, I shared that I needed some design and marketing help for our chiropractic business. He quickly referred me to the agency those three individuals owned and set up a meeting for that next week. In the first meeting, I met with Casey Harbertson and shared information about our products and what I needed help with. Through our conversation, Casey let me know that they primarily worked with companies in the hunting industry and shared with me his passion for the outdoors. As we discussed, we found that there could be a great opportunity for our supplements in the hunting industry, and that if our products worked well, we could combine their marketing skills and abilities to really create something unique. A few days later, I met Casey's brother Jordan and their partner Joel Pilcher, and with excitement for what we all felt could be a very special opportunity to improve lives, we began the process of exploring a partnership together. Each of us felt as though God had orchestrated this business opportunity to meet the needs and desires we all personally had for the business. But even greater than our own personal desires and needs, there was a great opportunity to improve and transform the lives of individuals and families in all that we decided to do and be at MTN OPS, and that became the sole mission.

I gave the guys some of the products that Nick and I had been selling through doctors' offices for years (that products in the MTN OPS lineup are known as Enduro and Yeti) and asked them to put them to the test in the mountains. I remember one of them calling me, and he couldn't believe how much faster he could hike without increasing his heart rate. The product was working for them! I knew it would, yet it was incredible for me to hear their excitement. From there, the process of branding and establishing the business began.

The marketing team worked hard to create the actual MTN OPS brand, name, and look and feel. But I think we can all agree that Joel Pilcher knocked it out of the park with his design of our MTN OPS logo and icon. We immediately had something that everyone wanted to wear. It's not often that you wear your nutrition company's shirts and hats, but once we launched, everyone wanted to.

I had never hunted before MTN OPS, so I did not know the passion that existed in the life of a hunter. I have since found out, but for those who don't know, let me explain. The average hunter may spend 7-10 days actually hunting each year. The other 358 days they will spend preparing, dreaming about, talking of, and rehashing stories over those days in the field and the memories made until it is time to get back out. It is a passion I can't adequately put into words, but I'll try later through my own experiences and hunts that I share in Phase Six of this book.

Think about what it is in life that would make you want to get up out of bed at 4:00 a.m. Not a lot comes to mind, but for a hunter, they know. Not only are they willing to wake up at 4:00 a.m., they are up and hiking through the dark in all kinds of weather conditions, all for the passion of the hunt. At the time, I couldn't quite understand this, but when I saw the look in the eyes of those who hunt as they shared stories with me, I knew it was something I wanted to experience, too.

There were two trains of thought for me: First, I could experience something entirely new, challenge my body, and see new parts of Utah and even the world that I hadn't explored before. Two, I could see firsthand how our products were boosting experienced hunters, a market I had never thought of tapping into that MTN OPS was now entering into full force.

Still, I was very much behind the scenes at first. I didn't need, nor will I ever care to have, the spotlight. But until that point, nobody really knew who I was, and I liked it that way because I couldn't speak the hunting language, nor did I have the stories to tell. That would quickly become the past as I truly have now found the passion myself.

After all, I'd just managed to break free of years of floundering. For so long, Jenna and I constantly worked to keep our heads above water. We prayed; we fought for air, and through the grace of God and our own tenacity, we could now *breathe*. That wasn't something I'd ever take for granted. We have invested our all into MTN OPS, owning our "stick-to-it-ness" every day.

As I jumped headfirst into the outdoor and hunting markets, I found individuals with whom I had much in common. We all had goals, dreams, and ambitions for life. One of those goals and dreams was that of providing for family, and I had now found an incredible way to remove some of the hunger we once faced by providing food that we would now harvest on the mountain. Conquering hunger now took on a new and incredible meaning, and the method was the hunt.

My connection to this incredible hunting community grew as I found people who also desired to be physically, spiritually, and mentally strong. Our social connections with each other created bonds of strength, oftentimes created in the outdoors and among God's creations. These bonds allowed not only me but all those who join our MTN OPS family to truly connect and conquer in a genuine and unique way.

Like any sport, hunting requires participants to train, focus, and be mentally and physically fit for the activity required. When hunters aren't in shape, their experience can be cut short of its full potential. Because of this, I quickly found a passion for fueling this newfound passion of mine and the community we now served, allowing hunters to do what they love doing longer and in a more enjoyable way.

In February of 2016, I got a call from my brother-in-law who offered me the opportunity of a lifetime. He and his father had purchased a South Africa hunt for four at a hunting banquet but were unable to go. They asked if I'd like to trade them some MTN OPS products for the hunt. *South Africa, what?* I hadn't been out hunting in the United States or even Utah yet, but I thought, *man if I'm going to go, I might as well GO BIG!*

"Well, YES!" I answered, totally pumped up. However, immediately upon my answer, the separation anxiety and fear of heights I'd suffered with on and off since childhood began to plague my mind. Night and day, all I could think about was being that far away from my family—and being up in the air for that long flight! It would take four hours just to reach Atlanta and then sixteen hours to Johannesburg. Still, I swallowed my anxieties and began to plan the trip of a lifetime. It was only a couple of months away, and there was so much to prepare for. I didn't even have a passport, so we expedited that process and paid a pretty penny to get it there on time.

The days leading up to the hunt gave me every excuse to just stay home and in my comfort zone. As I drove around the neighborhood with my daughter, Hallie, who was twelve-years-old, she asked if we could play our song while we drove. She, too, was experiencing some severe separation anxiety, knowing I would be so far away. When she cried (and I wanted to), we said a prayer together. I was so nervous and asking the most bizarre questions trying to prepare that I think even my friends wondered if I would show up at the airport. But what almost kept me from really leaving was Kenzie, who was nine at the time.

Jenna and I had decided she couldn't wait. She needed to get her tonsils out right away. Jenna was fine with my trip as long as I was at home for a few days after the surgery to make sure all was well and Kenzie was healing. This wasn't a simple tonsillectomy; Kenzie hadn't been getting enough oxygen in her sleep, and without this and some other intensive surgical repairs to her bite and jaw, they would have had to completely reconstruct my daughter's jaw to make sure her facial bones could continue to grow normally. It had to happen and quickly.

Fortunately, the surgery went well, and we were at home with Kenzie as she rested and recovered. The next day, however, just one day before I was to leave for South Africa, Kenzie's throat began to bleed. In fact, she bled into her stomach for a while before we knew what was happening. All we knew was that suddenly she became very sick, and we rushed her to the hospital as she had started throwing up blood. Nearly every other fear and anxiety I had ever experienced paled in comparison. I could barely keep it together as Kenzie and Jenna were rushed back into the ER.

I parked the car as quickly as I could and raced to her room. As I rounded the corner, I couldn't believe the scene before my eyes. There was blood everywhere. They could not stop the vomiting, and it seemed to be all blood. At the end of Kenzie's bed sat a blood transfusion kit. Just the day before, Kenzie was worried about being put under anesthesia for her first round of tonsil removal, but now was almost begging to be put under to find some sense of relief from the intensity of pain. We said a prayer, and a quick blessing was pronounced upon her, and they wheeled her away to have her wounds cauterized.

I immediately told Jenna that I could not leave to do something so much for myself when my daughter was home experiencing this. Leaving my wife to handle it on her own did not seem fair. Jenna knew my anxieties and had helped me through them in the past. She was not about to let me miss out on this opportunity and insisted that everything would be ok and that I should go.

The confidence in her eyes and words calmed my anxieties. When the surgery was over, the doctor came to tell us that everything was fine. I told him I was to go to Africa the next morning but didn't feel right leaving my daughter this way. I remember him saying, "She will be much more excited to hear your stories of Africa and the adventure than she will be to have you sitting next to her on the couch for the next week." Jenna again agreed with a *see I told you so!* look in her eyes, and with that, I recommitted to the adventure.

Some very close friends decided to join me for the hunt, and the next morning I met them at the airport for what would soon be a major turning point in my life. I know it is not possible for everyone to do this, but I wish that every beginning hunter could start in Africa. It is a target-rich environment and helped me come to understand how I would feel taking the life of an animal and consuming it.

In the end, it helped me gain an appreciation for those I would spend time with, that truly being my greatest passion within the hunt, the time with wonderful people. No distractions, no cell phones, no noise from the world. Just you, sometimes a guide, some friends, family, God's creations, and God. I fell in love with what hunting could do not just for the relationships with the hunters I found myself with but, most importantly, with God.

Despite our gracious hosts, the first two nights there I didn't sleep. On one hand, I couldn't stop thinking about my family, especially Kenzie. She was doing so much better, but I was prayerful that they would all be okay with me so far away. (Really, I think we all know it was me that needed prayers, being so far away from them.) On the other hand, I stayed up through the night just listening to all the sounds of Africa, the baboons with their barks, the jackals with their high-pitched howls, the vast number of birds and their distinct calls; this was the voice of Africa, surrounding me in my little thatched roof bungalow. There was a world I had never experienced before right outside my door, and I was so excited to immerse myself in it.

We woke up early that first morning to all the sounds of African animals surrounding us. After a quick breakfast as the sun rose, I anxiously waited for our hunting guides to be ready to go out in search of our first animal. I was well equipped with my first set of camo, my first hunting boots, and my first and brand new Hoyt bow. There was an energy and excitement in the air that, without question, I could feel. I conjured up in my head exactly how I thought the hunt would go down, the African savannah, the dangers that might lurk in the underbrush, the desire to avoid the lethal black mamba. But then, once we were out and on foot, everything I thought I would see and experience went out the window. I was in the moment, experiencing only what was actually right in front of me.

About an hour into our hunt, there they were. Off in the distance, I spotted a small herd of blue wildebeests. Within the herd was an old mature bull, which became my target. The hunt was on! The adrenaline rush was more real than I anticipated as we stalked into a good distance for a shot. I had the big bull in the crosshairs. *What a beautiful animal,* I thought to myself as I watched him through my scope. He was black colored, but as the sun hit his hide, there were almost golden stripes that appeared.

That was the moment I was most curious about when it came to discovering whether I could pull the trigger and take the life of an animal. Breathing now took on an all-important meaning. I needed to breathe calmly and intentionally so that I could ultimately settle in and calm my nerves to take a good and accurate shot.

The goal was for the wildebeest to take its last breath as quickly as possible, with as little suffering as possible. To me, an ethical, accurate, and quick harvest was the priority, and I did not take it lightly. With that, my first shot, on my first animal, was complete and successful.

I approached the bull with respect and great emotion. To be right there next to it and up close was breathtaking. Photos were taken to remember the experience and the story that we would share with friends and family. I experienced a deep feeling of gratitude knowing that this meat would now go to a family in need. I knew what it was like to be a family in need of nourishment, and being in Africa, there were plenty of families who could benefit from this harvest.

I was able to appreciate now, on a different level, the cycle of life giving life. Nothing from this or any of the other animals was wasted; all was or would be consumed by us as hunters, by the families we shared the hunt with, and my personal favorite, by the community we were able to donate meat to. What a humbling experience to visit a South African orphanage and deliver meat we harvested that would now be consumed by needy families and orphan children who would savor this incredible gift and life-sustaining support.

We told the outfitters in advance that on Sunday, we would love to find a way to a church. They knew of one in town and gladly offered to take us, and they even attended with us.

Arriving shortly after the meeting started at the small church building in Mokopane, South Africa, we could hear one of "our" hymns being sung by the congregation. It was a different language, but the music, the feelings, and the spirit behind what I was hearing was palpable. Sheer joy overcame me. We sat with the congregation, who welcomed us with big smiles.

A young boy, probably seven years old, sat next to me and shared his hymnal. Every few seconds, he would look up into my eyes to catch a glimpse of this American sitting next to him. I'd give him a big grin, and he'd hurry and look the other way. I don't remember the messages shared in that small chapel that day, but I do remember what I felt, especially the passion that accompanied the words and messages of those who spoke.

This gospel was everything to them, and it was everything to me. We were brothers and sisters from two sides of the world, yet we spoke, felt, and believed the same things. God brought us all together, and that connection with these people was the highlight of my hunt.

Kenzie's doctor was right. She and all my kids loved hearing of my adventures in a place all the way around the world. There were moments that felt like forever, when I missed my family, yet when all was said and done, the adventure was over in the blink of an eye. I had overcome some fears and my separation anxiety, and by so doing was able to demonstrate to my children that they, too, can overcome those things that cause them fear and to experience the many opportunities that oftentimes come our way.

I knew I was now just getting started into a passion and a lifestyle that would bring adventure, memories, perspective, travel, connection, and a new breath of life into my family's journey. I also knew that if I was going to do this, my family would come with me as much as possible. To experience these incredible adventures for me just would not be the same without them by my side.

As I write this book, eight-plus years after the launch of this mission-driven brand, MTN OPS, I contemplate the blessing of being able to go to work each day with a team, product, brand, and mission that centers fully around improving lives. I am beyond grateful to be a small part of the equation, especially knowing what it has done to improve my own life.

We have broken down so many walls and opened our doors to the lives of those who want to join our MTN OPS family. Connection is what our brand is all about. But many don't get to see all the inner workings of our team, so I'd like to give you a little glimpse into what you'd experience walking into MTN OPS every day.

I call it our *Conquer Culture,* and conquering is what our MTN OPS culture is all about. There are four core elements of our conquer culture:

1. Core Values: Our decision-making guardrails.
2. Customs: Our traditions and routines.
3. Connections: Our relationships and interactions.
4. Commitments: The expectations and responsibilities we have for one another and for the brand.

Every week at MTN OPS, you will find the team gathered for our weekly huddle. The week and this huddle always start with a prayer, recognizing God (our number one core value), and a blessing upon the efforts of the week. Someone from the team shares a thought on the core value of the month, stories of how each of us has conquered in life are shared, and expectations for the week are set.

Every Tuesday, the team gathers at midday for our Conquer Book Club and, following the book club, we all share a lunch together provided by the company. We believe in learning from one another and from the books we read as a company to better enable us to improve the lives of our customers. Being a valuable source of strength to conquer for our customers is of the utmost importance to our entire team. But we can't give what we don't have, and so we put team building and training at the top of our priority list.

Every Wednesday at MTN OPS, our team meets for meditation, breathing exercises, and a cold plunge in the four ice baths at our HQ. This process helps to focus and ground us in our work at the office and our work in life. The well-being of our team and their families is first and foremost. The MTN OPS team is, without question, the secret sauce to the success of our company and the connections we build within our community. Some of the most incredibly talented, passionate, and motivating individuals I have ever met are key contributors to the success of our mission at MTN OPS. They have become ***family,*** and my first and foremost stewardship is to make sure they are valued for their contributions and have all the

opportunity for growth they could ***desire*** as they choose to devote to the brand. I highlighted and italicized three words—Family, Opportunity, and Desire—in that last sentence because those are core values of the brand that I will dive into later in Phase Seven but that make a huge difference in the experience our team has working together at MTN OPS. We are a safe place for our team to test, learn, and apply all things we are passionately committed to learning and executing upon. Ultimately, people are safe to be themselves, and we seek to learn and know the strengths of one another so that we can not only celebrate those strengths but focus on putting them to maximum use to propel the mission forward.

The MTN OPS office is located on a mountain road. Fitting, right? The building is the old historic Rock Loft building in Fruit Heights, Utah, built into the mountain and constructed to process all the cherries from the cherry orchards back in the mid-1900s. We have equipped the rock and timber structure with a 3,000 square foot gym for employees, friends, and family to take advantage of in their pursuits to conquer more physically. The MTN OPS team has dedicated themselves to a monthly Conquer More challenge internally, where our focus on the physical improvements of healthy living is emphasized. Many team members, including three of our sales leaders, have gone through major physical transformations of their own. Those three sales leaders have lost over one hundred and twenty pounds combined, and the benefits that have come are not only physical but social, spiritual, and mental as well. They have been incredible assets in their progress and success at MTN OPS and in life.

On an almost weekly basis at the MTN OPS HQ, we hold smaller Operation Conquer Hunger service projects where youth groups, sports teams, families, and other corporate groups come to help us assemble pantry packs for school children in need. This is a small portion of what we do but a large portion of who we are. To me, the work that occurs within the walls of that building is sacred and truly focused on improving a life—one person, one meal, one transformation, one connection at a time.

At our very first hunt expo in 2015, we worked with the Diesel Brothers to build an awesome, souped-up Ford Truck we called "THE BUCK

TRUCK." We gave that truck away in our "TRUCK FOR A BUCK" give-away with the Diesel Brothers. The truck took up our entire 20'x20' booth.

Everyone loved the truck and started asking, who is MTN OPS? Our booth was swarming with people. If they bought our shirts and put them on right then, we discounted the t-shirt by $5, and we pretty much sold out of shirts. Not only did that work great for revenue, but the entire expo hall had thousands of people walking around with this new MTN OPS brand, and we took it by storm.

At that first hunt expo, we had a world champion arm wrestler, Jarod Cash, there with his arm wrestling table, and if you could beat him, you won a free product. Not many products were given away that day. Have you seen his arms?

Even a world champion gets tired, and so when he would rest, I would take my place at the arm-wrestling station. It was during those intervals that product began to walk off for free. My arms were sore, so sore that I couldn't even pick up my one-year-old when I got home from the expo that night. That is when I learned how powerful our Phenix muscle recovery product truly is.

The next year, in 2016, our booth got a little bigger. I think we went with a 40'x40'. In 2017, it was even bigger with a 30'x60'. In 2018, 40'x80' followed up in 2019 and 2020 with what I believe was a 100'x40' booth. We offered MTN OPS celebrity ambassador signature opportunities, where you'd find a lineup lasting two hours, giving our customers an opportunity to meet those who inspire them, such as

- Cameron Hanes: An iconic bowhunter, endurance athlete, author, husband, and father.
- Eva Shockey: An exemplary mother, wife, author, lifestyle blogger, and hype-woman for all things outdoors.
- Jim Shockey: The legendary Canadian outdoor writer, professional big game outfitter, television producer, host for many hunting shows, husband, and father.

- HUSH: A team of passionate hunters who have built a brand and community on YouTube and social media to inspire, educate, and give back to the hunting community they love.
- Corey Jacobsen: An 11-time RMEF World Elk Calling Champion and the founder of elk101.com, husband, and father.
- Brian Call: A hunter, conservationist, public land defender, host of the Gritty Podcast, husband, and father.
- Justin Martin: An American businessman and reality television personality from the reality show Duck Dynasty, husband, and father.

During these hunt expos, we hold our own after-parties, always making them family-friendly. We also hold our annual Cam Hanes/MTN OPS KEEP HAMMERING 5K on one of the most beautiful routes around the Salt Lake Capitol.

Outside of the hunt expo, we gather for large-scale Operation Conquer Hunger events three to four times per year, allowing our customers to gather and serve by building pantry packs for those less fortunate in our community. If you want to give people an opportunity to build trust and feel a part of an experience, then I always recommend serving with one another. Nothing brings people together more than suffering through something together, especially when it is for the good of another. Service is key to creating a great experience.

As we looked back over the experiences we have had interacting with our customers, especially the in-person interaction at events such as the hunt expo, we noticed something truly transformative happening. At the first hunt expo we exhibited at, we were overwhelmed by the number of people who would pull out their phones and show us their "kill shot" from the previous year's hunts. The giant bull or the incredible buck that they were able to harvest. We had a blast hearing their stories and sharing some of our own. Although at the time of the first hunt expo, I had not yet even hunted, so I was basically hearing everyone else's amazing experiences. Oftentimes, their experiences felt so very similar, one story to another, yet for each person telling the story, it was different because it was their own.

Contrast that with our second hunt expo in 2016. We were overcome with emotion, gratitude, and amazement by the new stories that we were being told. At the 2016 expo, individuals would come up to us and pull out their phone. We expected to see another kill shot photo of an incredible animal, but oftentimes with tears in our eyes, what was presented to us was their "killed it" photo. It was their before and after photos from their personal and physical transformation that year. They had connected with us throughout the year; they committed to our product and the healthy living lifestyle we promoted, and their lives began to change. The tears well up inside as I think of certain individuals who had this experience, and there were many. They would show us these photos with tears streaming down their faces, setting off the tears in our eyes and in the middle of an expo hall swarming with people. Just picture it: much of the time, these were bearded, masculine men with sweaty eyes in the middle of the MTN OPS booth, sharing a transformative experience with one another and connecting in a way that has had an incredible impact on lives in areas of life that matter most. Tears of gratitude, hugs of thanks, and expressions of love have been shared in those many and sacred moments.

These experiences continue to this day, with thousands of Brand Ambassadors sharing their heartfelt appreciation for the community, the brand, the products and the people who have transformed their lives. I truly stand amazed that God would bless me with this opportunity to be a part of the journey of His sons and daughters as they seek to take care of this asset, their bodies, that He has given them in which to house their spirits in this mortal life. It is a stewardship and a responsibility I do not take lightly, nor does any member of our team at MTN OPS.

With that said, I feel and will always feel that MTN OPS is much more than a business. It is a mission, and it is backed by God, influenced by goodness, and tracked by transformations and the improvement of lives. When God is with us, who can be against us? Well, while you'd like to think that everything would just be smooth sailing when you are trying to do what is right, it seems that the adversary takes special interest in those involved in transformation.

Humans have the remarkable ability to make choices. That is the greatest gift that God has given us: the ability to choose. Breath is that moment between stimulus and response, and we were built to breathe in a way that allows us to make the right choice in our efforts to conquer more. But that doesn't mean that the choice is always easy. It's what differentiates us from animals. It's also what can overcome fear, anxiety, ego, divisiveness, and greed. While I still have struggles, I have been able to overcome so many and love that every day I can now choose to breathe in a different and impactful way.

We were meant to conquer more! How? We were built to breathe. We were built to learn and make better choices and let everything we've experienced in life be the training for making better and better choices in our bodies for our families and for our communities. This is how we conquer.

JOY IN THE JOURNEY

I was recently at a funeral of a dear friend. His children stood and spoke of his life and the journeys his life took him on. As his daughter spoke, I was astounded when she mentioned my mother and a simple quote she would always remind us of growing up: "Find joy in the journey." To understand the destination is important, but to find joy in the journey along the way is truly a task and challenge to focus on while learning to conquer the mountains in our lives.

My mother always taught us as children—and even now as grown children—that joy comes from focusing on "joy" as an acronym. To find joy, we focus on Jesus, Others, and Yourself, all three needing our attention. I have found this method to be true and spot-on in my life.

Russel M. Nelson states "The JOY we feel in life has little to do with the circumstances of our lives and everything to do with the FOCUS of our lives."

For me, when I look back at the financial suffering we endured as a couple and a family facing that seemingly impossible mountain, I ask myself, *would I be okay doing that again?* Without hesitation, if it meant being an instrument in God's hands to bring a life or a soul unto Him and His unsurpassable joy, I would do it a thousand times over.

The learnings and opportunities that knock on our door during the experiences we are given in life are incredible. They should not be taken for granted. So often we look at the rough times as something to *endure*, to somehow make it through, waiting patiently for the storm to pass.

I have another thought: What if these are our moments to become what He needs us to become?

From the words of Russell Bruson, "What if everything you're going through is preparing you for what you asked for?"

What are those things you ask, seek, and knock for God to open unto you? Maybe He is helping you become what you need to be for those blessings to be ever-present and ever appreciated in your life.

PHASE 5 CONQUER CHALLENGE

Seek an ability to breathe more freely, both spiritually and physically, and find joy in the journey by combining an intentional prayer with fasting. Below, write down a date you will fast, the purpose of your fast, and following the fast write down how you felt both physically, spiritually, and mentally. What did you learn, how were you tested and how did you breathe?

____

____

____

____

____

____

____

____

____

____

____

____

____

____

____

____

PHASE 6

BUILT FOR THE HUNT

"Behold, I will send for many fishers, saith the Lord, and they shall fish them; and after will I send for many hunters, and they shall hunt them from every mountain, and from every hill, and out of the holes of the rocks. For mine eyes are upon all their ways: they are not hid from my face."

—JEREMIAH 16:16-17

The commitment. The adrenaline. The fear. The thrill. The adventure. The elements. The sweat. **The finish line.**

The commitment. The adrenaline. The fear. The thrill. The adventure. The elements. The sweat. **The harvest.**

I couldn't believe it when I finally realized it. All the components that marathoners strove for and hunters lived for were so much the same—the planning, preparation, strategy, gear, and nutrition to survive the elements, all committed to achieving a new personal best.

In my friend Kevin Hall's book, Aspire!, he speaks of the word PATH-FINDER. "In speaking of a leader, the first part of the word Lea means Path and the second part of the word Der means Finder, a Leader is a Pathfinder. A Leader is a pathfinder, they find the path. They are a reader of the signs and the clues. They see and show the way."

In his book, Kevin asks a question: "Could you imagine a hunting party going out in ancient days? Those who become the leaders see the sign of the game and stop to listen. They pause to catch their breath and get on their hands and knees to recognize the clues. They see the hoof marks; they are the ones with the best hearing who put their ears to the ground and listen to where the game is. They are the ones who touch the ground and can tell which direction the animal is traveling. In olden times, finding the true path of the game was life-sustaining. Being a leader means finding the path. But before you can help someone else find their path, you must know yours."

So now, as I prepared for my Moab marathon each day, I started early, and each day felt like a hunt! I had a target in mind, and that was being in top physical condition to run the marathon to the best of my ability. I had to train my body to get into a routine that was not just physical but mental and spiritual on most and many occasions. My day started with discipline; waking early, studying my scriptures, and then heading out the door to hunt down the physical attention my body needed to succeed.

This was the goal; this was my purpose; this was my hunt.

I AM THE PIONEER

I am the pioneer of hunting in my immediate family. My grandfathers and one uncle hunted and fished, but then it kind of skipped a generation. As I dove headfirst into the world of hunting, I found that it was so much more than I ever anticipated, to the point that it became paramount for me to involve my entire family. Right away I was surprised to find just how much it enriched all my relationships with family and friends.

As I fell in love with hunting, I found, to my amazement, that there are many kinds of hunters: rifle hunters, bow hunters, big game hunters, waterfowl hunters, upland game hunters, whitetail hunters . . . the list goes on and on.

While many pick a specialty, some hunters do it all—and I know plenty who do. They may hunt for a variety of different reasons, but many include the relationships that are built around hunting, the adventure, the freedom of land, the stewardship and conservation of wildlife and land, and for many, it is to obtain and provide clean and healthy protein for their families. While I have heard of some, I have yet to meet a hunter who is only in it for the trophy. Almost every hunter I know has more respect for life, land, liberty, and family than most anyone I have ever met. There is a great respect for the animal and the life-giving-life essence that occurs on a hunt.

From what I have experienced, all I know is that every hunt is filled with lessons, many of them life-changing and unforgettable.

FIRED UP OVER THE FIRE BULL

The night before exhibiting at our first Hunt Expo in February 2015, I drove with a friend to the first-ever HUSH movie night in Salt Lake City. This movie night would be an opportunity for the HUSH team to display their hunts from that year on the big screen at a movie theatre. MTN OPS was sponsoring the event, and I was actually quite excited to see my first-ever hunting film.

I did not know what to expect and didn't know if I'd even like it, but I was just excited to be experiencing something new. As we drove to the movie, the friend I was with said something to the effect of "Don't get your hopes up. Oftentimes, these hunt films can be a bit boring." We found our seats in the movie theatre, which was not huge but probably held two hundred people, and it was packed with not a single seat available. There was an energy in the room that was electric, and everyone waited in anticipation for the films to be shown.

I watched as two very passionate hunters, Eric Chesser and Casey Butler, educated and entertained their audience with self-filmed experiences that evoked many emotions. There was laughter and there were tears, there was defeat and there was triumph. There was respect for the animals that they both hunted and harvested. It was not this bloodthirsty scene with no respect for life. There might have been more respect for life in these scenes than most anything I had seen from entertainment.

I was truly in awe and respected what they had taught me. Eric's *FIRE BULL* film especially got me fired up. As I shared with Eric and Casey later,

"What you did was give me a glimpse into what it was to be a hunter, a conservationist, a steward over God's land and creations! I'm amazed."

Looking at their grinning faces, I could tell they were encouraged by what their films had stirred within my soul and especially the desire I was now feeling to become a hunter. Something deep inside of me, especially from that moment, told me I needed to learn, and I needed to get out and do what these guys had done.

That is when it all started.

THE HUNTS

BUCK AND A TRUCK
Fall of 2016

My first year putting in for the hunt draw in Utah was 2016. Utah uses a point system to reward their tags to applicants. If you don't draw that year, your points build up, gaining you preference for future draw opportunities. In most cases, it does not take as long to draw an archery tag as it does a rifle tag because there just aren't as many bow hunters as there are rifle hunters. I just happened to draw my archery mule deer tag that first year. This was my first hunt since returning home from my South Africa adventure. I knew the wildlife wouldn't be as abundant as Africa here in Utah, and still, I went with archery as my method of choice and with that, the odds of finding something worth shooting were greatly diminished. In the end, for me it really is not about the kill; it is about the experience; it is about the adventure.

I set out on my second hunt, this time in my own backyard of Utah. The plan was to take my two oldest daughters, Hallie (twelve) and Kenzie (nine), with me and spend some time together in the mountains hunting for mule deer from a Thursday to a Saturday night. My wife and I had purchased an old 1972 camper trailer from a friend of ours for $350, and I pulled this behind my wife's SUV so that we would have somewhere nice and warm to sleep, seeing that the crisp fall nights were now upon us. We were all packed up, and off we went, ready for adventure.

Our hunting area was only about one hour away from home. About five minutes before we got to camp, along the side of the road we saw one buck and three doe. The buck was a small two-point, but still it was a buck! And he just stood there, about forty yards off the road staring at us, making no movement.

What do I do? I thought to myself. I quickly took a photo of the buck and sent it off in a text to the guys at the office. My text along with the photo asked:

Should I go after this buck?

They wrote back:

Get out of the car and get him.

I quickly jumped out of the SUV, slammed the door, and heard my phone buzz again.

Make sure to not slam your door.

Too late! But that buck did not move.

I looked at my daughters and said, "This will end our trip almost before it begins. Are you okay if I take this deer?" They both responded with an excited yes, a bit surprised that it was already happening.

Knowing that the success rate of getting a deer with a bow was very slim, seeing this buck not move, having my daughters there to experience it all with me, and their excited response brought me to my decision to proceed.

I handed my phone to Hallie and told her to film. I still hadn't gotten my bow out of the back of the SUV. I didn't have my release on yet. A release is a trigger device strapped to your wrist that helps to release arrows from the bowstring rather than the from archer's fingers. I had to go digging through some bags to find it, and this all took time. I was anxious for him not to run . . . but still, the buck just stood in place.

Finally, I was ready. I drew back on my bow, took a few deep breaths, pulled the release, and off the arrow went. Where would you guess that buck went? Luck was on my side that evening because he ran directly to the road just thirty yards back from where we were, laid down in the middle of it, and quickly expired. It was a quick and ethical shot. I could not believe what had just happened, and neither could my daughters. We looked at each other in disbelief. They looked at each other, and then they looked back at me, excitement in their eyes and smiles from ear to ear. We had discussed this part of the hunt on many occasions, building up to it. I would often say *the chances of actually getting a dear with a bow on my first hunt will be extremely unlikely and difficult*, so I don't think we even believed it would happen, but it just did.

Now, the real work began. First, I had to back that tiny trailer nearer the animal, which ended up being one of the harder things to do that night as that trailer was so squirrely on that narrow dirt road. We finally got the trailer to the animal, pulled the buck off the road, took some photos with my daughters to record the experience, and then the girls looked at me as if to say, "Now what?"

Oh yeah. Now what?

Honestly, I hadn't been trained in the art of gutting and dressing an animal by myself yet. I again texted my friends a photo of our buck. Was I embarrassed? Yes! I should have known what to do, but quite honestly, I didn't think I'd even have an opportunity to shoot a buck! I certainly didn't expect to be gutting and skinning one within forty minutes of leaving home.

I was grateful my friends were super supportive. "You aren't too far," they said, and I could imagine them chuckling. "Just head back this way and we will meet you at your house to take care of everything." I don't think it crossed their minds that I didn't own a truck yet. I had always wanted a truck but had not yet arrived at that point of manhood.

With the help of my daughters, we spread out some plastic tablecloths in the back of my wife's nice SUV, and together we hoisted that heavy buck up into the back. Looking at each other cringing just a little, we started our trek back home. This time, we drove with windows down and shirts over our noses. In that SUV, it smelled like the world was coming to an end. We couldn't arrive home soon enough. Pulling in the driveway quietly, we placed the buck at the doorstep and rang the doorbell.

Jenna opened the door completely and utterly shocked to find a deer lying outside the house. She let out a quick gasp and then started to chuckle. My daughters were so proud and excited to surprise their mother. Beckham's first reaction was, "Well, that's small." That was true, but the experience was huge for us. I had just successfully harvested my first archery mule deer. With the help of friends and business partners, we got every bit of meat off that deer that we possibly could.

As this occurred, I waited for a question from my wife that I knew was coming: "Wait, how did you get this buck home?"

That's when I said, "Well, we just laid him in the back of your car."

Her response could not have been more priceless—nor more harmonious to my ears. "You need to get yourself a truck," and that I did.

Within about two weeks, I had my first truck, and man, was my testosterone roaring! My first buck and my first truck.

In hunting, in business, and just in our everyday lives, there are opportunities presented to us. Like my little buck, it may not be what we had imagined. Would I have liked an opportunity at a giant buck? Yes, but sometimes, the shots we take in life come at us a little differently than we had imagined. Many times, our first shots are smaller opportunities that lead to bigger and bigger opportunities until what we had imagined comes to pass, or, at times, it happens in an even greater way than we imagined.

BUCK AND A TRUCK HUNT LESSONS LEARNED:

- To take opportunities when they are given to us, no matter how big or small. Often the small shots we get in life lead to much great shots in the future.
- While this is often a male-dominated activity, I knew my daughters were up for adventure, and they enjoyed every minute of our time together. I was able to find something new in the outdoors that we could do to spend quality time together. These shared experiences strengthened our connection to each other.

- Having good friends surrounding you who can say, "Yes, go get it" is a gift. Surround yourself with those who encourage you to take the leap, grab an arrow, and let it fly.
- Lastly, if you need or want a truck, take your wife's car on your next hunt and bring a buck home in it. If she is as smart as Jenna, she will know that if something doesn't change history, it will be sure to repeat itself. Go get a truck for your next buck.

COMMUNICATION IS KEY - ESPECIALLY ON A BEAR HUNT

JUNE 2017

I have a very healthy fear of bears. But in June of 2017, not even a year after our last archery deer hunt and with my new truck, I decided there would be no better way to confront that fear than by spending some time in the woods with them. To add a few more elements to my challenge, I did not go alone but again took my hunting partners and daughters, Hallie and Kenzie. It's one thing to fear something, but then to take two precious daughters into facing that terror with you definitely put my anxious mind and heart on heightened alert. The amazing thing about this hunt was that I would not be the only one hunting; in fact, the focus would be on Hallie and Kenzie having their first tags. After only one hunt with me the year prior, they both wanted to take a shot of their own, and now was the time.

What impressed me most about my daughters was their trust in me. They were scared, too, but they trusted and followed me as we conquered the fear together.

Fortunately, I was smart enough to know that the three of us newbies could be dangerous alone. I had a great friend named Ben who offered to support us in this hunt. Ben was an avid bear and mountain lion hunter. He had basically lived amongst the bear with no worry whatsoever of the danger we felt we were confronting. Ben's confidence, his knowledge, and his time spent amongst these wild animals put my worried heart at ease. I would call Ben multiple times to have him walk me through how the hunt would work. I'd ask Ben questions like:

What does it look like where we hunt?

Do we have to hike far?

How close to the bears would we actually be?

Can we be further away than that? I laughed.

Finally, in late spring of 2017, my daughters and I set out on the road to Idaho. We again pulled our 1972 camper, but this time it was pulled behind my new truck. I absolutely loved having a truck, and my truck loved hunting, off-roading, and pulling our little old camper trailer on each of these adventures. The camper was a private place to escape to on this hunt, but we found through a few nights of rainfall that the roof needed repair. For three nights straight, we soaked up the rain inside of our trailer, and my daughters were the greatest sports soaking it up with smiles on their faces.

I will always remember the confidence and joy in my daughters' countenances and in the way they hiked up the mountain toward the tree stand we would sit in. While I hiked the trail in trepidation and fear, they hiked like conquerors up the mountain, full of faith and confidence. I remember thinking to myself how happy they both looked and how excited they both seemed at the prospect of potentially seeing a bear. We were there for four nights, and every day around four o'clock in the afternoon, we hiked the same path, the girls following Ben and me behind them. I watched them enjoying the moment and trusting not only in their father, but maybe even more so in their guide, whom I, as their father, trusted.

I didn't have good hunting gear for them at the time, and we were still scratching our way out of the financial burdens we had been in, so buying new hunting gear for kids who were growing quickly was not at the top of our list. With that said, a good friend and owner of Kings Camo had given me a great deal on some of their entry-level kids' gear, and with that, my daughters could at least blend into the trees. With the girls growing so quickly, their new camo was already shrinking in size, but they seemed grateful and content to have their own gear. I felt horrible when the rain started coming down because I did not have boots for them. They each had a pair of tennis shoes for this hunt, which did not keep the water out. As they sat with wet feet in the tree stand, I honestly can't remember either of them complaining one bit.

We were deep into the woods, and our attention was completely on each other. Each of the girls expressed appreciation and excitement to be there with me at least a couple times, and we did our best to just be with each other in the moment. I felt that even though I had my own anxieties about hunting bears, we were able to fully enjoy the time with each other and to be present as we walked up the mountain, sat in the tree stand, and anticipated seeing a bear come into the area we were set up in.

That first night, we were blessed to have Ben sit in the tree stand with us, and man, was I sure glad. We sat on high alert, as still as possible, waiting for any sign of a bear. Toward the end of that night, having sat in the tree stand for a few hours, I had honestly started to doze off. As I was in and out of sleep, I felt a nudge from one of the girls, and my eyes opened to see a bear walking across the hillside in front of us. My adrenaline went through the roof. We were thirty to forty yards away from a bear for the first time in our lives. Hallie was all setup and ready with her rifle, which was laid across the safety bar to the tree stand in front of us. The safety bar made for a great gun rest. I had taken the girls shooting many times in preparation for this hunt, and each of them was an excellent shot. Hallie controlled her breathing, and with the pull of a trigger, Hallie had a successful harvest. I have found that many hunters use the word harvest instead of kill as a way to speak with respect for the animal whose life was taken. It truly is a harvest of wonderful meat that our family and friends enjoy. I was so proud of how calm Hallie stayed when the bear came in and as she got ready to take her shot. Once the bear was on the ground, we were high fiving with excitement, and ultimately, respect. We lowered ourselves down the tree stand ladder, and I watched with appreciation for the respect Hallie had toward the animal.

The second night was radically different than the first because our guide left us to sit alone. He hiked up to the tree stand with us, made sure we were settled in, gave us a radio, and told us to call him if we had success; otherwise, he would come back for us at dark. With that, he slowly disappeared down the trail into the woods. Yes, we were all worried. Suddenly, I could tell by their body language that my daughters were not confident because of me; they had been confident because of our *guide*. I was in their same shoes.

The three of us had been sitting for a short time up in the tree stand when in the distance, I could see a bear working its way toward where we were sitting. I quickly but stealthy leaned over a whispered to Kenzie.

You need to get ready. A bear is coming.

"Right now?" She replied.

Yes, he was headed right this direction up through the trees, you'll see him in just a moment.

Kenzie took in a deep breath.

We all began to shake with excitement. After only a few minutes, the bear made its way into the forty-yard distance from where we were. Kenzie was ready; she steadied the rifle, found the bear in the scope, waited for the bear to stop broadside, and with a deep breath and an exhale, the trigger was pulled. Her shot was accurate and quick. I was so proud of her for the accuracy of her first harvest and at the age of only ten. She was so calm and collected, just like Hallie. I quickly radioed our guide, Ben, to let him know we had a bear down, but there was no response. We sat for a bit and called on the radio again, but again, there was no response.

There was a bear down below us that we knew had expired, but with all the signs of bears we had been seeing, the scat (bear poop), the tracks along the trail, the fact that we saw these two bears in two nights, as well as the information we gathered from Ben, we were sure there were others surrounding us. Even if they weren't surrounding us, it sure felt like the mountains had eyes on us the entire time. I wasn't sure what to do, so we decided to climb down the tree stand and make our way down the path to where the truck had dropped us off.

It was one mile to where the truck dropped us and another eight miles down the deep, dark forest to make our way back to camp. I did not want to make that long journey, especially in the dark, and my hope was that Ben was waiting for us after that first mile. With my rifle in hand and two anxious young girls by my side, we made our way down the path, frequently trying to reach Ben on the radio but still no response. I felt a little panic inside, not knowing whether Ben would be at the bottom of the one-mile hike. Hallie shared that she, too, was panicking inside, each of us watching in every direction for signs of bear. Kenzie, on the other hand, seemed to be a bit more confident, more reassured because she was there with her dad and everything would be ok. I think she was also riding the high that just came from her first hunt.

When we got to the gate where the truck had dropped us, Ben was nowhere to be seen. There was a distress signal on the radio I was pushing in hopes that it might contact Ben or at least give him something to hear. Every time I pressed that button for the distress signal, it made a sound very much like a bird, almost a songbird of some sort. The radio would make the sound, and then I would hear a response off in the trees. I called for Ben but no response. Again, I sent the signal, and again, I heard the same signal responding in the trees, and after doing this for a few minutes, I realized there was a mockingjay in the trees responding to my signal and mimicking the same sound, an actual bird that was sending me a message in response to my signal, but it was not Ben.

At this point, we didn't know what to do, but we couldn't leave the bear up there, so we quickly, in the rain and with high anxiety, made our way back up the mile trail and back to our tree stand. I asked the girls how they were doing, and they were fine, just a bit worried. They wanted to climb back up into the safety of the tree stand, so that is where we headed. Fortunately, it was almost dark, and our hope was that Ben would soon be there to help us. Each of us said a little prayer that we wouldn't have to make our way down the nine miles to camp after having dressed a bear while in heavily populated bear country and now in the rain. At this point, nothing sounded worse or scarier than this. But I sat in that tree stand with my two daughters and knew

I needed to be brave for them. I prayed out loud so they could hear my trust in God, and I prayed that my daughters would be able to sit in comfort, to enjoy the beauty that surrounded them, and that we would soon be able to get down the mountain. To keep our minds occupied, we rehashed both of their hunts, sharing the feelings that went through each of them as they saw bears so close and how they felt as they looked through the rifle's scope. They could not wait to share the stories with their mom and with their friends, who were going to be so surprised that they had ventured out into the bear woods and lived to tell the incredible stories.

As the light of day began to disappear, the trees began to cast more shadows on the ground. The forest that once looked thick was now even thicker in the darkness, and the lack of visibility caused you to wonder what might be lurking in it. Our prayers were answered as, right at dark, we saw a headlamp coming in our direction. It was Ben, and wow did my heart take courage. I could tell that Hallie's and Kenzie's did, too, by the look of relief on their faces and the audible sighs they let out. With excitement, we shouted to Ben, "We got a bear." Ben also let out a sigh of relief and excitement and then asked, "Why didn't you call on the radio?" I told him we had been trying to reach him for some time, and as we compared radio dials, we realized that I was not on the right channel or frequency.

I must have turned it without knowing. Ben was not far from where we were, just a short distance on the other side of the canyon, but far enough not to hear the shot. With a new feeling of relief and excitement for the adventure of the night, we made our way back down to the truck, both girls having had a successful hunt.

Our car ride home from this hunt gave us a great opportunity to process all that had transpired. We talked about Hallie being the oldest sister and leading by example as she took the opportunity to hunt first on this trip. Kenzie is her little sister, and she looks up to her and wants to be like her. I was proud of the example Hallie set for Kenzie, and even in the moments that caused us some fear and anxiety, she did a great job at staying confident to keep Kenzie calm and confident. We especially enjoyed talking about the night of Kenzie's hunt, how Ben had left us alone, how our radio was not working, feelings of fear and panic, how we thought we would have to hike through the night in the thick forest nine miles to get back to camp. We felt that our friend and guide had actually left us alone.

There were so many parallels to this experience and life and much to be learned. One of which was how well we are communicating to our Guide, or our Heavenly Father, our God. Are we on the right channel? Is our communication clear, and do we even communicate at all? As we let out the distress signal, there was something out there in the woods mimicking our call, and how often does the adversary use his evil ways to mimic what we might be trying to find in life, bringing us a false sense of security and confidence, only to find out that the source of the sound is not the right or true sound at all. When our guide says he will come, just wait where you are. Do we patiently wait where we are, even though there might be dangers surrounding us?

When it comes to communication with God, there is, in a bible dictionary under the word "Prayer," one of the most incredible definitions and descriptions of what prayer/communication with God truly is and should become for each of us. Let me share it here with you:

> "As soon as we learn the true relationship in which we stand toward God (namely, God is our Father, and we are His children), then at once prayer becomes natural and instinctive on our part (Matt. 7:7–11). Many of the so-called difficulties about prayer arise from forgetting this relationship. Prayer is the act by which the will of the Father and the will of the child are brought into correspondence with each other. The object of prayer is not to change the will of God but to secure for ourselves and for others blessings that God is already willing to grant but that are made conditional on our asking for them. Blessings require some work or effort on our part before we can obtain them. Prayer is a form of work and is an appointed means for obtaining the highest of all blessings."

KING JAMES BIBLE DICTIONARY "PRAYER"

I have to remind myself regularly as I pray to truly speak to Him as though He is there because in all reality, He is! I know He hears us, and I desperately want to hear Him and often have in my life. As a father to my children, I want nothing more than for you to speak to Him, communicate with Him, and hear Him regularly in your life. Nothing will guide you safely home through the dangerous and oftentimes scary paths of life quite like being on the same channel, so to speak to Him.

I recently found a talk my daughter Kenzie gave in church, as a ten-year-old, shortly after this hunt. Here is a small portion of what she shared from that hunt and how she personally likened the experience to life.

"Earlier this summer, I went on a bear hunt with my dad, and each day, we would come to a gate. Behind that gate was a very narrow pathway that led us to where we needed to go. Our guide told us to make sure to stay on this path. If we left the path, there were dangers all around.

Especially when it got dark, we had to make sure to stay on the path in order to safely return home.

"Life is much like this path and even after baptism, there may be dark times, and there may be dangers. But if we stay true to our baptism promises, God will always be with us and bless us along the way."

Wise words from a ten-year-old. Life's experiences are often the greatest tools for learning, and I have found that when sharing those experiences with others, it becomes ingrained into what and who we truly are.

BUILT FOR THE HUNT LESSONS LEARNED:

- A trusted friend or guide in life can make all the difference.
- When it comes to communicating with a higher power, even God, make sure we are on the right channel.
- It doesn't take the best gear to make an amazing experience. It takes a good attitude and being in the moment.

PERSISTENCE IS KEY

AUGUST 2019

"It's a dangerous business, Frodo, going out your door. You step onto the road, and if you don't keep your feet, there's no knowing where you might be swept off to."

—J.R.R. Tolkien, The Lord of the Rings

It had been just one year since I had answered the call to adventure with my wife and two daughters on a caribou hunt in Alaska. I never could have imagined earlier in our marriage marriage we would have taken this type of adventure, but we answered the call and loved it. Jenna had experienced her first hunt in the interior of Alaska, where only the bold and the brave dare to venture, and I was so proud of her and the girls for their daring.

With an open invitation from my friend Jon to come back anytime, even every year, I took him up on it with a "Father and Son" adventure just one year later. This time, it was Beckham's turn, just having turned ten years old—the official hunting age in Alaska. When I told him, Beckham was all about it. Not only would I have my son there for his first hunt, but it was also my fifteen-year-old nephew Braden's first hunt. The icing on the cake? My friend Joe would also be experiencing his first hunt.

I had found so much joy in hunting that to me, I wanted to share it with everyone—like a good movie, or a really good meal, or better yet, like the gospel; once you have experienced it for yourself and love it, the next thing you want to do is share it and experience it with others who have yet to experience it themselves. I had such a newness and excitement still flowing through me from my life-changing hunting experiences.

I didn't even need to be the one hunting anymore; the excitement for me came from witnessing the thrill and joy and adventure. It was addictive to watch others succeed, watch them stretch, watch their adrenaline spike—and even sometimes their fear or surprise when they took up the courage to conquer more.

This Alaskan trip was an adventure. In contrast to the rainy weather in August just one year prior, I think we only had about thirty minutes of rain this entire trip. I grinned as I remembered just how soggy we had been. *The girls would have loved this weather!*

Just as before, we launched the boats into the river the first evening after arriving. However, with the weight of our gear and the number of people we had, we arrived at our desired destination in the dark. It was not the most comforting thing to be in one of these very shallow jet boats, traveling up a river in the Alaskan wilderness. The river presented new obstacles each day, and now traveling in the dark, we had our work cut out for us. But we arrived at the same base camp we were in with the girls after about a four-hour boat ride. Our expressions were that of exhaustion, but also excitement for what was to come.

As we traveled the river the next morning, we searched for signs of caribou along the shore and the riverbanks. We sought out meadows where the bedded animals had flattened the grass. Within a few hours, it was apparent that the herd had already been through the area, and we had missed them. This was not great news after having planned a trip like this for many months, done a lot of prep work, and with a camp full of excited first-time hunters. Truthfully, anxiousness set in, and I was disappointed that we would potentially miss the opportunity to hunt the way I had envisioned and expressed to my son, brother, nephew, and friends. But we did not just give up; never would we give up so easily. We would never give up on a hunt, especially one like this. But we did have to rework our plans and change locations to discover the herd.

There is never a hunt that goes exactly as planned. In the hunt and in life, we should always expect the unexpected. That does not mean our goal for the hunt changes; it just means that the path to get there might. Never change the plan; just adjust the course. Pivot when needed, but never give up on the goal.

With that said, we had a goal of finding the caribou, and that goal not only caused us to change our plan and course, but we had to pivot a lot to make it happen. We only had so much time in Alaska, and we were already down two days. We all met over breakfast to plan, and the plan required commitment and effort. We would have to drive up close to the Canadian border, enter into the mighty Yukon River, and try to get ahead of the herd. But that meant a twelve-hour drive to the Yukon and then who knows how long to get in front of the herd. Everyone decided we were committed. Hearing about this plan, I have to admit, giving up might have entered my mind for a moment, but seeing the excitement in my Beckham's eyes and the chance at an adventure we would have together, that thought was quickly replaced with, let's go!

We arrived at the Yukon River around four o'clock in the evening, which was not the ideal time, seeing that it would be dark soon. We were three days into a six-day hunt, and we had mainly been driving the river and road, not hunting. Let me remind you that there are no gas stations along the river. Once we were off, we were completely reliant upon what we had. If there was an emergency, we better had hope it's not so bad that our Garmin InReach connection isn't enough. There was a bit of concern on everyone's face as we prepared the boats and gear for the river. We calculated over and over how much gas we might need and almost left a few barrels in the trucks because of the heavy load we already carried in the boats, but thankfully, someone smart, a friend with us named Dale, insisted on us bringing *all* the gas we had. Thank goodness we did.

We were off. The boats moved slower than normal because of the weight they bore. Around eight that night, it began to get dark, and we were not even halfway to where we thought we needed to be. Not knowing this area of the river as well as our last location, Jon recommended we stop before it got too dark and said he felt good about a small island in the middle of the river, which had a nice gravel beach we could pull up to.

We saw a log on the beach we could tie up the boats to, and we went right for it. Upon jumping off onto the beach, we noticed a pile of wood had been chopped and stacked, ready for a fire. We saw a ring of stones where the fire could burn and an area of flat ground, a perfect fit for our two tents. We searched for footprints, signs of life, or signs from a previous camper, but we found none. No burnt wood, no ashes left in the fire ring, nothing. Almost without having to say anything, Jon and I looked at each other in complete exhaustion and gratitude at the miracle before us. To travel as far as we had, amidst the treachery of the river and the wild that surrounded us, we became extra exhausted because of the added vigilance required to survive. To have picked that exact area on the mighty Yukon to pull up and to have had it prepared and waiting for us was nothing short of a miracle. God is in the tiniest details of the details in this grandeur of life. With that, we had an incredible night's rest.

In the morning, we were off to our destination, but not before leaving that miracle of a spot on the river exactly how we found it in hopes that it might be found by another exhausted traveler in the future. Waking up on the river was breathtaking. The mountains and terrain of Alaska are so vast and big that it is hard to describe without being there. It is a masterpiece of the creator that just goes on and on, as far as the eye can see and beyond. We traveled up a finger of the river toward the area we decided to hunt. We drove as far back as I thought any human had ever been. So far, in fact, we were jumping rock bars to get there. After traveling as far as we could, Jon asked Beckham, Andy (our videographer), and me to jump out to hunt this area. After we jumped out, Jon took off in the boat and headed back in the direction we had come to find another place for the other hunters to hunt.

As I watched the boat leave, panic struck immediately. I felt as small as I have ever felt in a huge wilderness. Fear found its place in me, as it distracted my heart and mind. Bear and wolf tracks were prevalent, and I had a hunting tag for both, but these tracks had to be those of grizzly, and that made things that much more worrisome for me. We found our way into some trees and found a great spot with a good vantage point to set up and wait in hopes that the caribou would cross our path. I was unsure what it was, but whenever we sat down to wait, Beckham would be asleep within seconds, and Andy usually wasn't far behind. I chuckled to myself as they both dozed off and prayed they wouldn't snore and scare all the wildlife away. I, on the other hand, was too wired to fall asleep. I did not want an opportunity to pass us by. Even when the odds are against me in the middle of the day to see an animal, I sit, I watch, I imagine it coming in, and I never rest. That is how I have been with a lot of things in life, and it may be a curse, but at times—especially on a hunt—I feel it has been a blessing.

Within a few hours, I could hear the boat coming back for us, and I sure was grateful to see it. We hadn't seen anything, and it sounded like the others hadn't either.

Finally, it was our last day in Alaska. As we gathered around our morning fire, enjoying our freeze-dried eggs and cheese breakfast, I looked at Beckham. He certainly wasn't ready to give up, and neither was I despite how we'd spent most of our time out here trekking through wilderness, nothing like what his sisters had experienced on their hunts.

We went to where one member of our group had gotten a caribou the previous day. Settling into a shaded spot along a rocky side of the river, we blended right in.

After merely two minutes, Beckham looked at me and yawned. Typical. Andy's eyes were drooping, too, like they were both so comfy out in the middle of nowhere that they needed a nap!

"Here's what's gonna happen," Beckham said as his eyes closed, "the caribou are gonna come down through those trees and cross the river there." He pointed about eighty yards away from us.

I nodded, thinking that was definitely possible. But when I opened my mouth to agree, my son was already snoring.

About half an hour went by, then . . . I froze. Out of the corner of my eye, I spotted movement. And it was exactly where Beckham had pointed!

"Wake up," I whispered, nudging my son and our videographer. "Look at that!"

We all stared, our breath collectively held, as a herd of thirty caribou came out of the trees to cross the water. Beckham had a beautiful bull in his sights within seconds, just like we'd taught him. When he was successful in his harvest, I grabbed him in a sideways hug.

Two major emotions flowed through me then, just as strongly as the Yukon River: one was excitement for my boy and his accomplishment, while the other was disappointment that, if we'd brought my nephew Braden along, he would have had the same opportunity. I felt awful that he hadn't stayed with us to reach his goal, too.

As we crossed the river to approach my son's caribou, Beckham was full of excitement. But what transpired next was what caused my father's heart to burst in joy over my son. Beckham knelt down beside the animal that was five times his size and Jon suggested we say a prayer. That's when Beckham spoke up and said, "I'd like to say it." After removing his cap, Beckham uttered one of the most honest, simple, and sincere prayers of gratitude to God:

> *Father in Heaven. Thank you for blessing us to be here in Alaska. Thank you for blessing us with this caribou that will feed us and others. Thank you for the safety that we have been given and for the chance to be together. We give you thanks in the name of Jesus Christ, amen.*

We all sat in reverence, recognizing the life-giving life of this animal, and we all were caught up in the amazement of this ten-year-old's maturity.

The evening hunt brought no results for my nephew, Braden. I was struggling to not think about and pray about anything else but that. Even my brother, Tyler, could tell that those were the thoughts and anxieties of my heart and mind. I wanted this for Braden more than just about anything at that moment. I carefully watched him to make sure he was feeling okay. He was quiet, and I think pondering on and hoping for success on this hunt. He was a young man who was out on an adventure and who desired to succeed. Braden is the type of young man who would have still been confident and okay had he not had a successful hunt but even more so because of his attitude of gratitude and humility and kindness, I wanted it for him even more.

I didn't sleep much that night because I knew we only had a few hours of hunting the next day before having to pack up camp to make our way back to civilization.

In the morning, Tyler, Braden, and Jon took off in the boat in one last attempt to find Braden a caribou. Beckham, Andy, and I were dropped upriver to watch for new signs of caribou or maybe even a wolf or bear. As we sat quietly, we prayed for Braden's success. A couple of hours had passed, and knowing they had to be out of time, I was worried about what to say to Braden if they had been unable to find anything suitable for his first harvest. As we sat on the riverside, I heard Jon's jet boat coming back in our direction. I sat up anxiously, waiting for their arrival. As the boat came flying around the corner up the river, all I saw were giant smiles on the faces of Jon, Tyler, and Braden, and I knew this meant success. In the final hours, the final minutes, or perhaps even the final seconds, they had succeeded because they never gave up. An overwhelming relief came over me; tears flowed freely; hugs were shared, and Tyler, with great emotion said, "I know what you have been feeling, brother. Thank you for your caring and concern." We all thanked God for the success.

Now, being midday and with at least a four-hour boat ride ahead of us and the need to still pick up camp, we took off in a hurry. The hunt was over, and we needed to make it back to civilization to catch a flight home the next day. We came out of the finger of the river in the late afternoon and started back up the Yukon, which was now flowing against us. Going upriver, but also having the load we now bore and just enough gas, we worked our way up the river. It was cold and starting to get dark. Jon was driving and had to stay as vigilant as he could to avoid any logs or sand bars along the way. One bad move and it could send us into the river, a river that doesn't bear the name the mighty Yukon for being weak. As we sat huddled in that small boat, we looked at each other and said, "This has been a high stakes hunt—and the adventure isn't over yet." There were a lot of things we needed to avoid and be careful of. I think I had been feeling that way the entire week and was ready to be safe on shore.

It felt like we would never arrive. The darker and longer it got, having passed almost seven hours in the boat, the more worried we all were. Then, in the midst of the worry, I saw Jon point up at the sky to one of the most beautiful sights I had ever seen in Alaska, the Northern Lights. We all gazed in awe. All of a sudden, as a Heavenly gift to distract us from our worries, we were intensely focused on the beautiful light show in the sky. Never had I seen anything like it, but gratefully they showed up for the last hour of our ride. For Jon these lights came as an answer to prayer, as well as lighting up the sky and the river we swiftly traveled upon. We traveled over 700 miles in jet boats during this trip, without any major incident. We made it back to shore, found the only motel in that little town, and in the morning, we made our way to the airport. What an adventure! What incredible miracles! What protection God granted us along our way. So many lessons were learned from this trip to Alaska, but maybe one more than the rest and that is that "God truly is in the details of the details." I saw His hand woven throughout that trip. In a world or a wilderness where we may feel as small as can be, the miracle is that God knows each of us individually. He will place chopped wood on the shore, create a ring for the fire to keep us warm, give a young man the success he desires, and light the way with the most beautiful lights to keep you going when it feels like the dark ride will never end. When all is said and done, God is our Father and will always show up in the little details of our lives. Had we given up along the way, with so many opportunities to do so, we would have never seen these great blessings and miracles.

BUILT FOR THE HUNT LESSONS LEARNED:

- Never give up.
- God is in the tiniest details.
- While we might feel small in this huge and vast universe, God knows each of us individually and will provide for us along the river of life.

"IT IS IN MY BLOOD" (ANCESTRAL CONNECTION)

SEPTEMBER 2020

"I went to the woods because I wished to live deliberately, to face only the essential facts of life, and see if I could not learn what it had to teach, and not, when I came to die, discover that I had not lived."

—Henry David Thoreau

I once saw a photo of my mother that shocked me. As a teenager, she was wearing a cowboy hat, a holstered gun at her waist, and holding up a pair of elk antlers! I couldn't believe it; yes, hunting had been part of Mom's upbringing via her father and brothers, but I knew she'd never harvested an animal herself. When I asked her about the photo, she said this:

"Oh, we took those after my dad got home. It was always so exciting when hunting season came around every year. I wish I could have gone myself."

Even though she was seventy-six when she said those things, her words stuck in my heart. As our family's newest hunting pioneer, I had to take her myself.

Holding her expression of desire to experience a hunt, I quietly went to work. Without her knowing, we arranged one of the greatest elk hunts she could ever experience in Utah. We purchased a tag for my mother from Western Skies Outfitters.

I was beyond excited to share the news with my mom that we had a hunt lined up for her. As we visited, I said, "Mom, Jenna, and I have an adventure planned just for you." Her eyes widened. "We are taking you and Dad on an elk hunt, and you will be the hunter!

She gasped, "Me? When will this happen, where will it happen, how will it happen?"

The questions came with great excitement and disbelief that she would actually have this opportunity.

We all laughed, cried, and hugged. She didn't have words, just emotion. She jumped right up and grabbed her "joy wand," a wand she created from ribbons and wrapping paper that she dances around the room with on birthdays, Christmas, and other special events to share her joy.

Then realization set in, and nervous excitement and more questions began to flow. She wanted to know all about elk, how we would use the meat, how rigorous the hunt would be, etc. The excitement again began to escalate as we painted a picture through words of what she might experience.

Her question about how rigorous the hunt would be was a good one because she wanted my father to be there with her. My dad just happened to have fallen twice during that same year, resulting in two broken hips, and he was not getting around as he once did. My typical elk hunting experience has been very rigorous, with a lot of hiking—hiking that typically took us deep into the forest.

Knowing my mother desperately wanted my father there but that he'd been using a walker, she and I weren't quite sure how well this hunt would go. But walkers and all, we were bound and determined to, if nothing else, just enjoy the outdoors together.

This hunt was like no other hunt I had ever been on, and I truly felt as though God was causing all the stars to align for my mother and father to experience this with Jenna and me. Gratefully, the outfitter had a ground blind, a type of tent for us to sit in and shoot from, set up over a small amount of water the elk would drink from. I was able to drive our side by side fairly close to the blind, allowing my father to not have to walk far.

It was a Thursday afternoon, the last week of September, and we had just made the one-and-a-half-hour drive from our home to the area in which we would hunt. After unloading our side-by-side from the trailer, we got our packs ready for an evening hunt. The guide had previously shown me where the ground blind had been set up and how to get there. I told my mom, "The animals typically bed down for the day in the shade of the trees, and so we will hunt them very early in the morning, before they go to bed down, and later in the evening just before dark as they are getting up to move toward their areas of eating and drinking. If we are to get into an area where they may go to eat or drink, we have to go early, sit in silence and patiently wait."

That is exactly what we did. It was about 3:30 p.m., and my parents, Jenna, and I were headed into the elk woods.

As we drove to the area where we would hunt, my mother was filled with great excitement and emotion. She spoke her feelings with these words:

"My father passed away years ago, and he loved to hunt. I can feel him close to me at this very moment. I remember the excitement from my brothers as they prepared to leave on the hunt with our father every year. I now understand their excitement. We all gathered in excitement to hear the stories as my father and brothers would come home from their deer and elk hunts, and I loved the amazing meals that were prepared from those animals. I am now feeling all those feelings. Trevor, this is in my blood." Immediately when she said that, I stopped the side-by-side.

"I have a special message I need to share with you from your brother Jerry," I said.

I had previously reached out to my Uncle Jerry, my mom's older brother, to see if he would surprise my mom and come on the hunt with us. Jerry is an avid hunter and one of the brothers I speak of who was always excited each year to get out on the hunt with his dad. Jerry wanted so badly to be there for my mother's first hunt, to surprise her, and to be there in support of his sweet sister. But Jerry had been battling cancer and was going the rounds with chemo and radiation at the time and wasn't feeling well enough to be there. I asked if he could record a short video message that I might share with my mom on her hunt, and that he did. When my mom said "Trevor, this is in my blood," I pulled out my phone and pulled up the video.

With great emotion from both brother and sister, we sat and heard a wonderful and encouraging message from my mother's brother to her. He spoke to her about the great elk, their massive size, and how many mouths it might feed. He also spoke of being out in God's creations and just soaking in the Spirit that we can connect with, He wished her success and, with tear-filled eyes, expressed his desire to have been there with her. Then he said, "Mary, this is in your blood."

I got everyone situated in the blind. Once situated, I drove the side by side back up and off the road a good distance and then made my way back to the group. It was now close to four in the evening. I shared some thoughts with my wife and parents:

"More than likely, we will be sitting until close to 8:00 p.m. tonight. I worried this would be hard for my father, whose hips were not feeling great. "The elk will not typically come into the water earlier unless there were extremely hot conditions causing them to work their way in earlier."

I got my mom set up with her rifle on some shooting sticks, and then we walked through potential scenarios for a few moments. She familiarized herself with the rifle, the scope, and all the little details. She felt ready.

Around 4:15 p.m. she was looking through the scope and started to say a little prayer out loud.

"Heavenly Father, we are here in the mountains, in Your beautiful creations. I am here with my husband, my son Trevor, and my daughter-in-love, Jenna. I love them. I am grateful for life. I am grateful for love. I am grateful for experiences that draw us closer to Thee. Heavenly Father, how exciting it would be to see an elk. What an experience it would be."

"There's an elk! Trevor, there's an elk!"

I thought it was just part of her prayer and didn't think anything of it, but then she said again, "Trevor . . . there is an elk."

I leaned up in my chair a bit to look through the opening in the blind and could not believe my eyes. At 4:19 p.m., after having only sat there for about twenty minutes, here came a giant bull elk out of the trees, heading to the water hole about sixty yards from us. The water was one hundred and ten yards away, the perfect distance for my mom to take an opportunity once he stopped. He was limping; something was wrong with a hoof. I could tell he was a big old bull, exactly what you'd *want* to find, especially if it is hurting from having fought with another bull, which is what they do during the rut. This was a lone Warrior Bull, having fought many battles, and with my mother's shot, he turned out to be a wonderful blessing to our entire family.

My mother was full of emotion as she approached that beautiful animal and continued her prayer of thanks to a God who not only provided but who provided in a way to make it possible for us to experience what we did—with my dad using a walker and all.

A few guides from the lodge came to help us with the animal. We dressed the elk with great respect, not sparing any meat. Then as a group, we gathered, and one of our guides, Cal, knelt down by the animal, asked us all to join, and like my mother, thanked God for the life-giving life and the opportunities of that day. We were all in tears with grateful hearts as we experienced this incredible hunt with my mother, my father, my wife, and other dear friends in camp.

My father said it best, "I have fallen in love with what hunting can do for relationships." This hunt was all about relationships. Relationships beyond the grave, relationships here and now, mother, father, son, daughter, brother, sister, God. I, too, have fallen in love with what hunting has and will continue to do for relationships I hold most dear in life.

BUILT FOR THE HUNT LESSONS LEARNED:

- Hunting can create a connection to those who have gone before. Allow it to do so in your life.
- As I ponder upon my ancestors, I connect with the fears they may have faced as they tried to provide. I connect it with the work it took for them to live and to survive.
- More than anything else on this hunt, I found great joy in introducing another female to the life of a hunter—my own mother, who had patiently and with excitement watched the men in her life at a young age experience the thrill of the hunt. But now, along with my wife, and my daughters, my mother was now built for the hunt.

AFRICA ROUND 2 - HUNTING WITH THE WHOLE FAMILY (JULY 2021)

"The majesty of this place soaks down to your bones and becomes a part of you; Ancient, Wild, Breathtaking. It is all of this, and much more"

—Tollies African Safaris

Ever since my first hunt in South Africa, I had been anxious to return so that my family could experience this great adventure.

Where to start with our family's South Africa Adventure? I am having a bit of writer's block as I ponder how incredible the experience was for us, and how to put in words our feelings from the adventure.

The day to depart finally arrived, and literally, as we sat in the airport ready to board our first flight, news on the television reported major riots in Johannesburg. My wife and I looked at each other, wondering if we should board the flight. I sent a Whatsapp message to my friend Paul in SA and asked if we were still ok to come. His response was that all was well where they were located, miles from the riots up in the mountains." If you didn't turn on the TV, you'd never even know what was going on."

We had about thirty-seven hours of travel, twenty-seven of which were actually in the air.

We arrived at the Eastern Cape of Port Elizabeth in the morning time, and our friends Paul Jordaan and his cousin, also Paul Jordaan, who went by the nickname Couzy, were there to pick us up in their awesome Toyota Landcruisers, fully equipped with benches and winches and all you would need for this hunting adventure. We arrived at their slice of Heaven on Earth later that day and were greeted by the rest of the Jordaan family.

We drove up the entryway to their property, the long, tree-lined driveway, the grove of trees their homestead sits within, the grassy lawn between bungalows that surround a beautiful pond from which the red letchway drinks morning and night. It truly was a slice of Heaven.

The Jordaan men are all athletes, and some are retired professional rugby players who had actually made a name for themselves in South Africa and France for their abilities. Each day for me began at 5:00 a.m. in their home gym where I was put through some of the hardest workouts of my life as we prepared for a day of adventure and hunting ahead of us.

Instead of recounting the details of the hunt, let me tell you of the wide variety of species we were able to see each day while in Africa. The kudu, which could be compared to our elk as the elk of Africa, is an elusive animal. But when you get a glance of their spiral horns, it is a sight to behold.

As we explored the land, we had not planned on seeing fallow deer, as they are not indigenous to South Africa. But we not only saw some, we saw some giants similar to what you might find in New Zealand or Australia. The loud baboons seemed to surround us in every direction, but they kept a safe distance. Thank goodness because these baboons were big and their canine teeth were larger than those of a lion. I learned fast that you do not want to cross the path of an angry baboon.

Nearly every day, we saw the beautiful springbok, the national animal in its variety of colors. The zebra, elephant, rhino, hippo, gemsbuck, and wildebeest were absolutely spectacular. Still, one of the sights that really struck all of us, especially my children, was watching a herd of giraffes move swiftly through the Savannah as if they were walking on clouds.

To see a herd of cape buffalo walking your way, not knowing you are just around the corner will cause the hair on the back of your neck to rise. Then, the warthog, with its tail sticking straight up as an indicator to its young followers to keep close, is so interesting to observe. The beautiful marks upon the body of the nyala left me in awe at the detail of that creation. The mere size of the eland bull at two thousand pounds will keep your attention. God truly let creativity flow when creating all that is South Africa.

But the people—the people who brought me to tears and will continue to take me back to Africa—are what will continue to take me back. Nothing is greater in Africa than the people. Our daily interactions and conversations with the wonderful Jordaan family always found their way to God.

In fact, the very first time I met Tollie Jordaan was here in Utah at the Western Hunt Expo sometime around 2017. He introduced himself to me by sharing a personal story that began with a cape buffalo wandering too close to their small town. One day, Tollie was attempting to corral that beast when it made its way through the gate in pursuit of him! Tollie, who was not able to outrun the buffalo, found himself being flipped like a rag doll, then continually pounded into the ground by the massive cape buffalo's horns that punctured Tollie's skin and a lung, and broke many bones.

Tollie's son, Paul, had just undergone major surgery, and he watched helplessly from a distance as his father's life was truly on the line underneath this gigantic and wild beast. Tollie mustered just enough strength to grab hold of the buffalo's horns while crying out, "God, if you need me, take me now; otherwise, let this buffalo go!"

As soon as he cried these words aloud, the buffalo stood up and walked away. Tollie ended up spending weeks in the hospital recovering from his wounds, but he would never forget the power of God during his near-death experience, and as he shared it with me, it left me in tears.

Learning not just of this story, but of Tollie's reasons for staying in Africa after receiving a life changing financial offer to come to the states, made me respect and admire this man and the way he led his family, community, and country even more. We both felt a connection and somehow a feeling of reconnection of brotherhood and friendship, as if we had known it before.

This family adventure to Africa was all filmed by our good friend Trevor Call. At the end of the twelve-day adventure, everyone was interviewed about their experience and what they loved most. In each of these interviews, my children always seemed to make mention of the Jordaan family they had come to love. However, my children also mentioned the day we spent in an orphanage.

I was grateful it was as deeply impactful to them as it was to me, this most sacred moment as I watched my children interact with children who have no family. Their eyes were opened to the contrast between the life they live and the lives of these young children, ranging from the ages of three to fourteen. The children of the orphanage danced for us, they sang for us, and we danced with them. We gave them simple gifts that brought some joy and excitement to their lives, such as socks, pajamas, beanies, food, and some candy. My children saw the circle of life, service, and love as they provided meat from their hunt to these hungry and needy children.

As we departed, I heard my daughter Hallie ask one of them if she could give them a hug, and suddenly there was a tidal wave of hugs as each child hugged and held tight to each of us for moments I wish I could hold onto forever. One little boy named Byron would not let Jenna and I go. We looked at each other with love and concern for this boy we did not know. The look in his eyes is burned into my memory.

I began this section with some text from a video done by my friends from Tollies' African Safaris. That text says, "What is it about this place? What is it that draws you here?" The animals, the spectacular views, the incredible food are all amazing, but for my family and me, it will always be *the people*. There are no coincidences in life, and the connection to the Jordaan family is one of those where God was in the details to bring us together. What is it about this place? The Jordaan family is, plain and simple. They are our family on the other side of the world.

BUILT FOR THE HUNT LESSONS LEARNED:

- Time and attention are so important for me, and experiences like these have become a great place to invest our time and attention.
- Connecting my children to amazing people around the world has enriched their life and given them a desire to know more about other cultures.
- We conquer as a family.

It is a beautiful thing that wherever you go, a hunting expo, a conversation with a friend on the mountain, a quiet prayer in a ground blind with your parents, or to the other side of the world you find people willing to talk about God and family and who teach you in their own ways about how to bring the beauty of both into the world. What an adventure God gives us to live.

In 2019, my wife and I had the privilege of spending a few days on Vancouver Island with Jim and Louise Shockey. Those familiar with Jim know that he is the Michael Jordan of hunting! Like many hunters, Jim is a devoted conservationist and steward of the land and an amazing golfer. Jim and his daughter,

Eva, have been ambassadors for MTN OPS, and it has truly been an honor to associate in a small way with them. What was meant to be an evening of dinner and filming Jim for a giveaway we were offering turned into a two-day retreat with a special VIP tour of Jim's "Hand of Man Museum"—truly a must-visit.

Along with the VIP tour, I got a first-class golf lesson from Jim himself. Man, was I embarrassed at my golfing ability! Still, he never made me feel small; he only instructed and built me up. His incredible wife welcomed us in, provided delicious home-cooked meals and took our wives out to the shops. What incredibly hospitable and welcoming people, who have devoted their lives to being pathfinders for others and to family.

Then it came time for filming. As the interview questions began, what I felt would potentially be a thirty-minute process ended up capturing almost two full hours of pure gold.

Jim spoke from the heart, shared his passion, and answered our questions with ease. At the end of the interview I asked, "You've been all around the world; you have hunted more animals than any human will ever be able to hunt in countries most of us have never even thought of traveling to. From all that you have done, what is your greatest accomplishment?" Jim looked straight into my eyes and stated: "You can look around at all the trophies, all the photos, all the artifacts, all the places I have been, and it *is* pretty spectacular. But I would say to those listening. Stop and smell the roses. Step outside and listen to a bird. There is a greater entity; look around you, there is a grand design in all of this. All of the things I have accomplished pale in comparison to what my wife and I have created with our family. Our greatest accomplishment is our family."

Jim's message was music to my ears. I can't stress enough the fact that hunters do hunt to consume and to provide, but the greatest opportunity for many in the hunting community is to build relationships through experiences with those we love.

I hope that you will feel the power that can be found in such simple experiences and that you, too, can see God's hand of teaching in your own life while you are out among his beautiful creations. During a hunt, a walk through nature, seeing, feeling, and hearing the beauty that surrounds me, I believe we need to take it all in and enjoy it, but I hope we find that those creations then turn our hearts, our minds, and our souls to the *Creator* of them all and that we focus on Him—and not just His creations. I feel strongly that this is what He would like us to do and that this is how we conquer.

PHASE 6 CONQUER CHALLENGE

What is a call to adventure you have been feeling? It does not need to be a hunt. It could be any call to experience this journey of life more fully. Write it down. What does it look like? When will it happen? Who will be there with you? What does it feel like? Now is the time to answer the call to adventure...

PHASE 7
BUILT TO CONQUER MORE

"I am come that they might have life, and that they might have it more abundantly"

—JOHN 10:10

The emotions ran freely as I crossed the finish line of my Moab trail marathon, but so did the exhaustion and pain. I literally sat there thinking, *How can anyone go any further?* I once thought the same about a marathon, and now my question has shifted dramatically: *How much farther can I go?* From that day on, I have been on a mission to Conquer more.

For the last six Phases of this book, we've gone on some big adventures together. After building our key foundation, we added strength and speed. Next came summiting the many mountains we face in life and learning how to breathe and be present during even the hardest of times. Through the surprisingly sentimental world of hunting, I've been taught some of this world's greatest lessons that I loved sharing with you.

But now we're moving onto the final piece, the magic of Phase 7: How can we create more with the mental, social, physical, and spiritual tools we've already journeyed through? Remember what we began with, readers: awakening the divine.

Let's dive into what that really means.

For me, it begins with honoring what we've accomplished today. After all, we can't Conquer More if we don't take a moment to breathe in what we currently have. Recognize that first, and then you can figure out where you can still go. Contemplate, recognize, and appreciate your current progress. Big or small, this step calls in gratitude for your abilities.

I love that the Savior speaks not just of abundance, but *more* abundance. Through him, our lives can be more abundant. Truly, because of Him, we have the ability to Conquer More than we ever could have imagined. When we started MTN OPS, our slogan was *Conquer Your Unknown,* and now it is *Conquer More*. But I love that there will always be more, even the unknown. What is unknown to us is known to Him, and so we must trust in His knowing.

I hope and pray that by learning to Conquer More in life, you will come to know the value of your life and truly awaken the divine.

To Conquer More is not complicated, and I am going to keep this section very simple to illustrate the point by sharing one quote that sums it all up by David A. Bednar. That quote says:

"If today you are a little bit better than you were yesterday, then that's enough. And, if tomorrow you are a little bit better than you were today, then that's enough."

A God who helps us in the process of Conquering More is pleased with the grateful soul who recognizes the good being achieved along the way. When we recognize the good, we recognize God!

CONQUER GRATITUDE CHALLENGE

Before diving into what you can do to do more, let's recognize what you are doing today that you are proud of. What are you doing well? What are you doing today that is better than yesterday? It is important in our pursuit to Conquer More that we recognize the good of today. Recognizing where we are at today will help us:

1. Recognize God by seeing Him within us and our improvement each day.
2. Recognize the baseline we should use as we work to improve upon tomorrow.

Celebrate four to five things you are conquering right now, today:

1.____

2.____

3.____

4.____

5.____

THE SECRET OF THE CONQUER CODE

"And Jesus increased in wisdom, and stature, and in favour with God and man"

—Luke 2:52 KJV

This scripture is the essence of The Conquer Code and the quadrants that are included. It seems to be showing up for me everywhere I look these days. "Jesus increased in wisdom (mental), and stature (physical), and in favour with God (spiritual) and man (social)."

Back in 2017, MTN OPS started what we now call our Conquer More Challenge. In the beginning, this was just for the team within the walls of the MTN OPS headquarters. We had no idea the incredible movement that was about to be birthed.

The genesis of this challenge was centered around the desire to truly live our mission to improve people's lives. But to help people conquer more in life, I believe you must also be conquering more in your own life. In other words, "You can't give what you don't have." So, if we are to help people conquer more in their lives, we must be doing it in our own.

With that said, we initiated a monthly Conquer More challenge. This challenge would not just be physical because at MTN OPS, we believe that wellness is not just physical but also pertains to spiritual, mental, and social aspects of life. And so, we began the challenge, each team member creating for themselves a set of goals within these Four Core Quadrants to gain long term and sustainable wellness in a balanced approach to life.

The first year was good. But it went from good to great the second year. Our customer service manager Candice recommended that we have accountability partners, and it truly did wonders. We went from a good amount of participation to almost 100 percent participation, as each member of our team was supported by an accountability partner to accomplish their goals each month.

New partners were then randomly assigned each quarter. At the end of every month, we drew names from those who had completed the challenge for prizes the team could win. To be entered into the drawings, you had to complete the challenge as a team. In our MTN OPS culture, we win and lose as a team, and this challenge was no different. Our culture of Conquer More really began to come alive.

My own children have adopted this Conquer Code to set and achieve goals for themselves. From my eighteen-year-old daughter down to my nine-year-old daughter, they are each accomplishing the great things they have set out to pursue. I have been blessed to catch them in the act of greatness, and I love it when I find my son, Beckham, getting a treadmill run in either early morning or late at night before he goes to bed to ensure that he can check off that physical box.

I have been incredibly proud of Hallie and Kenzie and the amount of good literature they are consuming and truly enjoying as they focus on conquering their Mental Quadrant task for the day. I am brought to tears as I walk into Savvy's room, sometimes late at night, to find her with a flashlight shining down on her scriptures, *finding the Lord* again and again in her Spiritual Quadrant of her day.

The scripture shared at the beginning of this chapter demonstrates the perfect example of our Savior and how He increased in these Four Core Quadrants as well. If we are to create a Code to Live by and Conquer by, I know no greater source than Jesus Christ Himself.

I invite you, your family, and your friends to join us and Conquer More by living The Conquer Code.

WHAT IS THE CONQUER CODE?

The Conquer Code is a ninety-day conquer more challenge that will help you build habits in the most important areas of life. My challenge to you is to truly commit. This is about you and for you. So often we look at integrity as something that pertains to our commitment and our word given to others, *but what about having integrity with yourself?*

We are the first to let ourselves off the hook when things get tough or schedules get difficult. When the going gets tough, those who conquer get going. I get it; everyone has bad days here or there, and there will be times when you fall short of your daily goal. Don't give yourself more than three strikes each month. As long as you have integrity with yourself and have truly committed, this should not be a problem.

So go out and Conquer More. I dare you to start *today*!

THE FIRST THIRTY DAYS

The first thirty days are all about building the foundation for this challenge. Each day, you'll do (one) task in each of the Four Quadrants, and as you progress into each phase, you'll essentially add another task to each day in those Four Quadrants. Here are your tasks for the next thirty days.

SPIRITUAL:

- Each day, commit to conquer by spending ten to fifteen minutes in prayer, meditation, scripture study, or a combination of these activities.

PHYSICAL:

- Each day, commit to conquer by spending thirty to forty-five minutes in physical activity. (Pick one day each week as a day of rest). If you need help with fitness ideas, you can find many free fitness programs to follow right at www.mtnops.com

MENTAL:

- Each day, commit to conquer by reading from a good book, listening to a good podcast, or by putting your mind to work while you learn something new.

SOCIAL:

- Commit to conquer by sharing something positive about your journey or just positivity in general on social media or in a text or email to a friend. Do this two times per week.

THE NEXT THIRTY DAYS

The next thirty days are all about building upon what you've done in the last thirty days and adding one additional task to each of the four quadrants for the next thirty days.

SPIRITUAL:

- Each day, commit to conquer by spending ten to fifteen minutes in prayer, meditation, scripture study, or a combination of these activities.
- Commit to Conquer through honesty in all that you do. If there are commitments you have made, follow through and be impeccable with your word. Use this or choose your own additional task.

PHYSICAL:

- Each day, commit to conquer by spending thirty to forty-five minutes in a physical activity. (Pick one day each week as a day of rest). If you need help with fitness ideas, you can find many free fitness programs to follow right at www.mtnops.com
- Commit to Conquer by adding one of the following tasks to your routine:
    - Take a weekly progress photo.
    - Improve your sleep: What would it take to add one more hour of rest to your life?
    - Drink enough water: Daily, it's recommended to consume 3.7 liters for most men and 2.7 liters for most women.
    - Follow a nutrition plan offered at MTN OPS.

MENTAL:

- Each day, commit to conquer by reading from a good book, listening to a good podcast, or putting your mind to work while you learn something new.
- Commit to Conquer by writing in a gratitude journal daily.

SOCIAL:

- Commit to conquer by sharing something positive about your journey or just positivity in general on social media or in a text or email to a friend. Do this two times per week.
- Commit to conquer by sending a thank-you letter once a week to someone who inspires you or someone who may need a little cheering up.

THE LAST THIRTY DAYS

You're a rockstar, and you already know what to do. For the next thirty days, you're going to come up with your own additional task to add to each Core Quadrant to accomplish.

SPIRITUAL:

- Each day, commit to conquer by spending ten to fifteen minutes in prayer, meditation, scripture study, or a combination of these activities.
- Commit to Conquer through honesty in all that you do. If there are commitments you have made, follow through and be impeccable with your word. Use this or choose your own additional task.
- Add your own 3rd task:

  ____

PHYSICAL:

- Each day, commit to conquer by spending thirty to forty-five minutes in physical activity. (Pick one day each week as a day of rest). If you need help with fitness ideas, you can find many free fitness programs to follow right at www.mtnops.com
- Commit to Conquer by adding one of the following tasks to your routine:
  - Take a weekly progress photo.
  - Improve your sleep: What would it take to add one more hour of rest to your life?
  - Drink enough water: Daily, it's recommended to consume 3.7 liters for most men and 2.7 liters for most women.

    - Follow a nutrition plan offered at MTN OPS.
- Add your own 3rd task:

____

MENTAL:

- Each day, commit to conquer by reading from a good book, listening to a good podcast, or putting your mind to work while you learn something new.
- Commit to Conquer by writing in a gratitude journal daily.
- Add your own 3rd task:

____

SOCIAL:

- Commit to conquer by sharing something positive about your journey or just positivity in general on social media or in a text or email to a friend. Do this two times per week.
- Commit to conquer by sending a thank-you letter once a week to someone who inspires you or someone who may need a little cheering up.
- Add your own 3rd task:

____

COMMIT TO CONQUER

Now that you understand the ninety days of your challenge, it is time to commit to conquering. Let's go!

I'd like to caution you against words like "someday." Instead, I invite you to accept this challenge today because of the immediate benefits you will see. If you aren't quite on board yet, that's okay. Here is where I'd love to offer you some examples from my own life.

This is what's happened to me personally since I've committed to Conquer More in the Four Core Quadrants. These stories range across many years of my life, so I hope they will provide the motivation you may need, no matter how old you are or how far you may think you need to go.

The point is, I struggled just like anyone else (that is something you know from the journey we've been on so far). There is a powerful peace that can be found in knowing where you want to go. Day by day, you can chip away at your goals and make all the difference.

SPIRITUAL QUADRANT

In the Bible, we learn that God created all things spiritual first before the physical. We are all spiritual beings having an earthly experience—not the other way around. In my daily attempts to live a conquering life, I stage my day according to this same sequence or pattern—and it's powerful.

As my alarm clock goes off in the morning, the first thing to hit the ground is not my feet. If you are young and sleep on the top bunk of a bunk bed, I would not recommend this, but if you are close to the ground, I would challenge everyone reading to roll out of bed onto your knees and begin the day in humble prayer. What does this tell your God about your priorities in life and where He stands? I have found when I first focus on Him, I gain His strength for the day ahead.

When it comes to prayer, I love the scripture in Matthew 7:7 which reads:

> "Ask, and it shall be given you; seek, and ye shall find; knock, and it shall be opened unto you".

As the Bible dictionary mentions in its section on prayer, much of what God desires to give to us as his children is contingent upon us asking, putting forth faith, and demonstrating our willingness to come to Him with those desires.

I personally love the "knock" reminder in this scripture and the thoughts it inspires within me. I have young teenagers in my home and, as you know, these youngsters like to play pranks—one of them being the Knock and Run, better known as doorbell ditching. I did plenty of this in my youth.

Late one weekend night and while scrolling through Facebook, I saw a post from one of my neighbors that said, "If you have been doorbell ditched tonight, here is your culprit." I burst out laughing at the doorbell camera photo of my nephew Braden in the act!

Braden and my daughter Hallie are great friends, so I assumed she would have been with him, but he was the only one caught on the camera! My neighbor did not know he was my nephew, but I took a screenshot of the post and sent it on to Braden's dad, my brother Tyler, and we had a good laugh. It was innocent fun. The neighbor kids loved going to this particular neighbor's house for these little pranks because this neighbor responded, and there is nothing greater than getting a reaction from your attempt.

Knocking at the door of the Lord is very similar. We can always expect a response, and it will always be the response we need, but maybe not always the response we want.

Let me share a few door approaches I feel we can use with the Lord as we *knock* and desire Him to open unto us.

First, there are those like my nephew who knock and run. At times, we all do this in our approach to prayer. We knock and start the prayer, but for whatever reason—whether we are distracted, don't know how to pray, or are scared to pray—we sometimes just run from the conversation altogether. It happens to us all and for varying reasons, but I pray we don't have this be a frequent approach.

There's been another, different prank attempt at my very door by teenagers I will not mention by last name, only Brock, Charlie, and Jake (I love these young men). With my own door camera, I am able to watch these attempts unfold. After the doorbell rings, I watch the mischievous boys crawl into sleeping bags on the porch and close themselves in, waiting for us to come to the door.

This has given me time to grab a hose and surprise them with a little water added to their slumber, and on one occasion, I snuck around the house and filmed them lying there in their three sleeping bags. As time passed, I heard them start to whisper one to another to ring the doorbell again.

One responded, "No, you go ring it."

"No, you go ring it!"

"He's got a lot of guns. You go ring it."

That made me laugh. I just let them talk amongst themselves for a time until they crawled out of their sleeping bags and were caught. We had some good laughs—that night and plenty since.

At times, our prayers can be a bit like this approach, where we stay there at the door but we sometimes go into hiding when the door is opened unto us. We don't express those feelings, desires, concerns, or questions of our hearts; instead, we wait and don't open up. For me, as a father, I love nothing more than when my children come to me and express the feelings in their hearts. I pray we will do the same: Come out of hiding and communicate to the Lord as He opens unto us.

Another approach I have seen is brilliant in its simplicity. We live amongst neighbors with very close relationships; oftentimes, these relationships are humor-filled. One time, our neighbor, a young teenager named Kennedi, knocked on our door and just stood there staring at us with no expression on her face. I actually pulled this one off as a youth as well. Just staring back at the person who opened the door, trying to evoke a response, hopefully a happy and laughing response and not one of anger.

This approach could very well be the best approach of them all. I'm as serious as the look on Kennedi's face. Truly, when was the last time you let the

Lord talk *first*? When was the last time you knocked in prayer and then sat quietly and patiently with faith, allowing the Lord to communicate to you? I've had some of my biggest breakthroughs with God when I have done just that. I invite you to allow time for the Lord to speak first.

Lastly, in the "knock and it shall be opened unto you" theme, there are the "Bigger or Better" parties. If you have never played this game, you have missed out! This game plays out by individuals splitting up into two teams or more. Each team starts with one object. It could be something as simple as a rock, a pencil, a rubber band—you name it. But you approach a neighbor's door and say, "We are having a bigger or better party, and we need something bigger or better than this. Are you willing to help? What might you trade for this that will help us win this game?"

The person at the door then takes your object/item and gives you something either bigger or better than what you presented them with. Ultimately, you come back together to find out what team ended up with the bigger or better items in comparison to what they started with. I couldn't believe it when my daughter Kenzie's team once finished the game with a TV. You just never know what you might end up with when you approach that door seeking something bigger or better.

When it comes to approaching the Lord, I can promise from personal experience that the Lord will always provide us with something much bigger *and* better than we could have ever imagined or come up with on our own! When we let God prevail in our life, it will always be bigger and better . . . because He is bigger and better than all.

As part of my morning routine, I spend ten to fifteen minutes in scripture study. This commitment has been a part of me for quite some time. As a teenager, I started my sophomore year of high school at 5 a.m. each day and was in the car by 5:30 a.m. to make the drive to early morning seminary for an hour-long dive into the gospel before heading off to school. This was incredibly difficult for one who struggled to wake up early, but I learned then that sacrifice brings forth the blessings we seek in life. I learned so much and did this for four years straight.

I'll never forget the first day of early morning seminary that year. Our teacher, Sister Peterson, challenged me to read the scriptures every day that school year without missing a single day. She told me that *if* I missed a day here or there, I could make it up by reading double the next day. She promised I would be blessed if I accepted her challenge. With that, I said yes and was committed!

Fast forward to my recent fortieth birthday. Although I accepted that year-long challenge by Sister Peterson twenty-five years ago, I have remained committed to this day! What an incredible blessing that sweet Sister Peterson's challenge has meant in my life. I do not share this to boast, only to share what a simple daily task can mean to any person at any age—and how simply committing to opening the pages of a sacred book each day of your life can mean all the difference.

When I was young, we sang these words of a primary song at church:

> **"Scripture power keeps me safe from sin.**
>
> **Scripture power is the power to win.**
>
> **Scripture power, every day I need,**
>
> **The power that I get each time I read."**

This power is exactly what I felt as a teenager, and I continue to feel it to this day. It was the power I needed to face difficult times and overcome temptations that definitely came—and continue to come—my way. Through daily scripture study, I can promise, just as Sister Peterson did to me, that I gain the power I need each time I read.

I challenge you to overcome this darkness and commotion by connecting on a spiritual level to your Creator every day. I challenge you to *commit to conquer* by spending time gaining the scripture power you need each time you read—and gift your children with this wonderful tool that will serve them all their lives, too. Seek. Knock. Open. Read. Conquer.

PHYSICAL QUADRANT

The physical quadrant will look different for everyone. You may have some exciting, new physical hobbies that you have committed your time to, or you may be at a stage of life where, for now, you find yourself unable to do what you once did. No matter where you are right now, it is perfect.

For me, the physical side of my journey has changed over time. I once watched my brother Trent train in the gym. He had the six pack abs, the buff chest, and well-defined biceps. I wondered how we were from the same gene pool.

I still don't have the six pack abs—at least they aren't visible. But I swear I can feel them. They say that abs are made in the kitchen, and I may love my donuts, cookies, and milk too much to ever reveal their existence! But there was a time when I physically challenged myself to become more well-defined and, more importantly, to gain additional physical strength.

For me, it started at a time when money was tight, back when Jenna and I were just getting our first supplement business started in 2010. I didn't like the gym scene—which was good because I couldn't afford a membership. Our business, combined with a few of my brothers' businesses, held an inner company physical challenge, and the winner would receive a prize of one thousand dollars. I needed the money and wanted to use it to take my family on a vacation. So, with some dumbbells and a bench in the warehouse of my brother's used car lot, I went to work every day with that thousand dollars in mind. Nothing was going to keep me from winning.

I did the same workout six days a week for three months straight. Most of the exercises focused on chest, shoulders, biceps, and triceps. I didn't have a friend to not let me skip leg day, so leg days were skipped for three months straight. Funny enough, I still have the legs to prove it, and I am glad the competition did not measure whether you were proportionate in your upper and lower body muscle and strength!

In the end, the hard work paid off, and I won the money. My winnings, combined with that garage sale we put on as a family, gave us enough money to take the kids to Disneyland. I not only had the financial reward for my effort and hard work, but I also had the energy to chase them around the theme park! Most importantly, I started to feel that my brother and I were indeed from the same gene pool (minus the six pack abs).

That routine of committing myself to something for three months stuck. Just like reading my scriptures every day, I was now taking greater care of the physical body God had blessed me with—and it felt great!

Growing up, I stayed physically active through sports. In my late twenties and into my thirties, I found great satisfaction in building additional strength and muscle through lifting weights. While I still love lifting, in my late thirties and forties, I loved discovering the endurance aspects and cardiovascular benefits of running, biking, and I hope to add some more swimming to the mix in the future.

In 1 Corinthians 6:19, it states: "What? Know ye not that your body is the temple of the Holy Ghost which is in you, which ye have of God, and ye are not your own?"

There came a point in my life where I had to ask myself what I was doing with this body, a gift from God that I had been given. I challenge you to *Conquer More Physically* through a daily routine of strengthening yourself and your miraculous body.

MENTAL QUADRANT

Like many people in the world, I still struggle with some strong anxiety at times. During a recent experience with elevated anxiety and feelings of inadequacy, a friend of mine recommended I print off the words to "The Serenity Prayer" and put them by my computer, nightstand, bathroom mirror, and anywhere I might be each day. The words of that prayer are as follows:

"God grant me the *serenity*
To accept the things I cannot change;
Courage to change the things I can;
And the *wisdom* to know the difference."

That was extremely helpful for me. But what mental fortitude and strength one must have to understand that some things are out of our control and we need to let them go. Finding the courage to change the things we can will bring about confidence and power in our lives. To know the difference between the two truly takes effect when we have gained wisdom. Wisdom comes through learning and experience.

For me, I have gained additional mental strength—something I still work on every day—by looking at my life's experiences and remembering how merciful God has been to me, how He has guided my path and helped me find the courage to take those next steps because I trust in Him. It's then that I take a step forward or a giant leap. I open the door and step through, and the mysteries of life and God's plan begin to unfold for me. Faith and trust have acquired special meaning to me in my life as so many of life's ponderables and unanswered questions have required that I move forward in faith *before* all the pieces fall into place. After all, I have learned that's what faith is.

There was a time in my life when getting on an airplane paralyzed me to the point that I sat at a few terminals within the airport and never boarded. Separation anxiety has gotten the best of me at times throughout my life. I have missed out on several experiences by not being willing—or in the moment able—to go.

But when I have found the mental strength to go outside my comfort zone and into that arena where there are things I cannot change or control, I let go of the wheel for just a bit. That's when I experience God prevailing with and for me in life, and I begin to *Conquer More Mentally*. I am no mental health expert, but I do know the Master Healer. My personal experience in life gives me confidence in saying that if we connect with Him, we will Conquer.

SOCIAL QUADRANT

In today's age, we lead such busy lives that, too often, our social connections fall by the wayside. As humans, we need social, face-to-face interaction to thrive—now more than ever.

In fact, connecting with others is more important than you may think. According to the Canadian Mental Health Association, "Social connection can lower anxiety and depression, help us regulate our emotions, lead to higher self-esteem and empathy, and actually improve our immune systems." Equally important, social connection can help us prosper in complex environments and teach us skills we wouldn't learn on our own.

Not only does social connection improve quality of life and boost mental health, but research has shown it can decrease the risk of suicide and actually help you live longer!

There is one other aspect that I have found when conquering social connections. They taught me to serve, to look outside of myself, and to find places where I could learn from others but also serve others. Learning to become outward-focused on teamwork and meeting needs in a group or community creates unity and a powerful feeling of tribe—an ancient need in the DNA of humans for survival! In the case of *Conquering More Socially,* this human connection not only combats fear and isolation, but it is also where miracles can happen. We become that for each other.

Some amazing friends of the MTN OPS community, including my brother Tyler, have created a special program sponsored by our company and carried out in the MTN OPS gym called *Connect and Conquer*. Through this program, we work with youth who may be struggling with high anxiety and depression, truly something we all face at some time in life and in varying degrees.

These youth are brought together in a social environment. "We" are always better than "me," so what great strength do we find through connection? In this program, we offer a variety of exposure exercises, where the youth are exposed to things that normally might cause them anxiety, like picking up a gigantic python. The youth then work together through a series of mental strengthening exercises. From there, they work physically in the gym for thirty minutes, being taught to strengthen and take care of their bodies and have fun. This allows them to be buoyed and strengthened by their social interactions in the group.

The long-lasting outcomes of the group have been that they feel connected, realize their feelings are normal, and find the strength to conquer more, having developed another set of life skills that will help them on their way.

Do you feel connected in life?

Where are you finding those connections?

Are they healthy or toxic?

Do your connections awaken the Divine within you, and are you able to be who you are truly meant to be or at least be on the path to becoming that person? Or are your connections doing the opposite?

I believe we all can know and feel where we are at with our connections in life and if they are enhancing our abilities and qualities or if they are diminishing those very gifts. Jim Rohn once said, "You are the average of the five people you spend the most time with." Who are these people in your life, how are these connections with them blessing you, and are you progressing with the help of these people to be the person you feel you are meant to be?

The path to connection is simple, but it takes courage and commitment to this quadrant of life, to Conquer More Socially. In the end, our time and attention to relationships and our service to others are what matter most.

COURAGE TO CONQUER

I have found it to be completely natural to lack courage or confidence when starting down the path of transformation. This pertains to not just the physical but all quadrants of life. You must know that you have it in you to reach above the lies that sometimes reside within your head and heart. You must know that you truly were born and built to conquer. One of our customers at MTN OPS wrote to tell us of his experience finding *courage* and *confidence* through Conquering More with us. He said:

> "Before my journey began, I had little to no confidence and even less self-worth. I spent my whole life being overweight and unhealthy. I had always wondered what it would be like to not be overweight, but I never put an effort to make the change.

> I tried to avoid public places. I never went swimming and at all costs would avoid pictures of myself. I reached a point where I felt if I didn't change, there would be health issues in my near future, which honestly terrified me. I never wanted my family to see me suffer due to my weight and health issues.
>
> When I joined my first Conquer Fitness Challenge (at MTN OPS), I couldn't bring myself to submit my before photos so I just started. Within a few short months, I felt like a completely different person. I had this smile that would never go away. I began to feel more confident in what I was doing, and that changed the perspective of my life which, in turn, changed my view on life. I'm not afraid to set goals anymore. I have the confidence to go to the gym or to a pool or even to submit my photos of myself for all to see and that is truly amazing to me.
>
> Thank you to all that supported me and a special thanks to all that doubted me. Your doubt helped push me far beyond what I thought was possible and pushed me to #CONQUER MORE."
>
> —Brian F.

When I think of our involvement in Brian's journey, I am extremely humbled that we played a small role in bringing about confidence in his life. It is amazing that he lost so much weight, but the fact that he has found confidence and a smile to go with it means the world to me. His transformation increases my desire to find others we can work with to bring a smile into their life.

There are many things in life I have had to find the *courage to conquer*. Many of those fears I have faced have come as I have spent time outdoors, with people who knew more than me and with God. The lessons learned have helped me understand how to not only face the challenges with *courage* but how to come off as a Conqueror.

One of those experiences occurred while sitting high up in a tree stand, a tree stand whose previous occupant might have been a five-hundred-pound black bear . . .

HIGHER GROUND

Sure, I continue to have some fears in life; two I've been forced to face head-on are the fear of heights and the fear of bears. Because I work in the outdoor and hunting industries, I have been confronted with both of these fears more times than I'd like! But having confronted them, I have experienced some incredible adventures. I have been in the wild within yards of these enormous creatures. I have also been on some very treacherous terrain in places like New Zealand, Africa, Alaska, and right here in my backyard in the Rocky Mountains of Utah. While all of these have been life-changing adventures, they have also maxed out my anxiety levels at times.

On an archery elk hunt in Utah's Wasatch Mountain Range in the fall of 2019, I was confronted with those two greatest fears—all in one experience! It was one of the last days of the hunt, and I had not had an opportunity to harvest an elk with my bow.

For those not familiar with bow hunting, you must be much closer to the animal than with a rifle. Because of this, it requires patience, stealthy movement, extreme silence, and the understanding that less than ten percent of archery hunts ever end in "success" with an animal harvest. It is not easy, but I think that is what draws me and countless others in.

On this day, we started hiking into a predetermined area where there were a few small puddles of water for the elk to drink. Near the water, up in a tree, sat two tree stands. The plan was for me and my videographer, Tyree, to sit in the tree stands from morning until night, if needed, for an opportunity to harvest a bull elk.

My knowledgeable friend Matt Davis led us there and pulled out his phone. I thought he was going to show me a prize bull elk they'd spotted nearby. After all, that was what I'd requested. Imagine the chills that raced up and down my spine as he showed me a picture of what looked like a five-hundred-pound black bear and then warned me that friends of his had recently seen this bear coming in and out of this exact area each day!

Oh great.

"I'm not showing him to you to scare you," Matt pointed out at the look on my face, which I am sure became completely devoid of color. Matt knew my extreme fear of bears. "I just want to make sure you're aware of what you *might* see. Just keep a lookout." He went on to add, "Don't worry, he won't mess with you if you don't mess with him." We both laughed. I couldn't help but notice that his was heartier than mine.

Matt then showed us the tree we would climb, about thirty feet in the air. At the base of the tall, quaking Aspen tree, I saw fresh claw marks. My gaze scaled up the tree, following the claw marks until they stopped—right at my tree stand! My anxiety kicked into high gear.

I pointed to the claw marks and looked at Matt questioningly. Matt laughed again and said, "Yes, bears like to climb up to investigate what is in the tree stand but not while you are in it. Just don't leave out any snacks or food." We all chuckled as he continued, "But be warned; what they like to do is tear any cloth they find to shreds."

I couldn't help but notice that the cloth that had been covering the seat I was supposed to sit on was ripped to pieces. I opened my mouth to tell Matt that was it. We would be hiking back out with him. But I tried to bury my fear, knowing I could conquer what I was feeling. With my pack on my back and bow in one hand, I slowly climbed the small hooks that had been twisted into the tree to allow our ascent.

To add insult to injury, as I climbed the tree and while Matt departed, he yelled, "One last thing: I forgot to bring my tree harnesses, so hold on tight and try not to fall!" That did nothing to boost my confidence, but I had already committed to conquer.

I was seated in my tree stand, and Tyree was seated in the same tree just a little above me, facing in a different direction. Someone had anchored a hook deep into the tree just over my right shoulder, where I was able to hang my pack, which was now securely attached to the tree. I checked the time on my watch, and it was about nine in the morning. Still, I was far from feeling settled in.

The downward slope of the canyon below me made everything feel much higher, which made me tremble already. What made this worse was the fact that there was a strong breeze making the tree sway back and forth. Every time I swayed above that downward slope, I felt like I was looking down three hundred feet.

I sat, white-knuckled, holding onto that small metal chair that barely fit my bottom, and I was not comfortable. In fact, the wind, the heights, and all that now surrounded me caused serious vertigo to set in. I began to feel dizzy and with that dizziness, nausea. My mind started to play tricks on me, and at times, I felt I was going to fall right out of that chair.

After about ten minutes of dealing with this, I turned to Tyree and told him the struggles I was facing and that I was not sure how much longer I would last. Tyree responded with a great idea. "Well, we could climb back down and build a ground blind in the trees to wait for the elk to come in down there."

"Great idea," I replied as my stomach roiled uneasily, "except for *the bear* that might come by!"

He laughed and said, "Well, I guess you'll have to choose your fear today."

Sheesh! Heights and nausea? Or bears and claws? This felt like a no-win situation.

Why am I a hunter? Why am I hunting? Why today? Why did Matt lead us here, of all places? Who cares about a harvest? I'll have to find another way to feed my family. My mind whirled.

I told Tyree that I would give it a little longer to see if I could find a way to get comfortable. Then I began to ask God to give me something that could help me feel secure and confident up in that tree. As I prayed, my eyes caught hold of the canyon floor, and I followed its ascent up and up until I was looking off to my right, where the canyon floor was now at my eye level just to the right of me.

Immediately as my perspective changed, the ground looked much closer to eye level, and a welcomed peace began to set in. Now, my prayer was of gratitude as I kept following the gradual slope of that canyon floor as it ascended behind me. As I continued to look over my right shoulder I found myself looking to *higher ground.* As soon as I was looking toat *higher ground,* complete confidence, peace, and comfort washed over me.

Since I would not be able to look over my shoulder all day long, every few minutes as my natural fears arose, I would focus my attention over my shoulder on *higher ground* to find my peace and strength.

Suddenly, I saw out of the corner of my eye the pack that I had attached to the tree. It was completely attached to the tree, but *I* was not. I had a sudden burst of inspiration. The pack had a strap, which I lengthened, threw it over my shoulder and then yanked down as hard as I could. Now I was also attached to the tree. Along with peace, confidence, comfort, and excitement began to grow. Even the breeze I once resented was now a welcome friend under the hot sun of the day. To my surprise and delight, suddenly, the views became unreal and beautiful, ceasing to be nauseating and scary.

Securely attached to this tree, my mind wandered to an experience my family and I had with our new friends, the Jordaan brothers, Paul and Pieter, from South Africa. They had arrived in Utah for another Hunt Expo and, at our invitation, stayed in our home. This is where we cemented an already beautiful friendship.

We invited them to join our family each day at 7:00 a.m. for scripture study, and each morning, we read passages of scripture referencing Jesus Christ. On the last day of their stay, I invited them to share something with my family as they departed. Pieter asked to use my Bible, and he turned to John 15. In his rich African accent, he read:

"'I am the true vine. I am the vine; ye are the branches.'"

He then looked up and tenderly locked eyes with each of my children and said, "What your father has taught you of Jesus Christ this week is true. He is true; He is the true vine, and we must attach ourselves to Him."

I rehearsed Pieter's words in my head as I now sat in this tree stand, attached to The Vine, and felt even more at peace.

We sat in that tree until 9:00 p.m. We endured the heat of the day, and we endured potential dangers and fears. The bear did come in but did us no harm. I remember seeing something move in the distance, and then he slowly entered the clearing, hopped up on a big fallen down tree, and sat on it for a few minutes. He looked about, as if to observe whether the area was safe, and then approached the water. He drank for a moment and then would look up, even in our direction at times, as if he knew we were there. After twenty minutes of just wandering the area with ease, he turned and walked out in the same direction he had come. What an amazing sight to see! I felt more excitement than anything and no real fear at all.

As what happens often in archery, I didn't get my elk, but in the end, Tyree and I endured. Once again, I marveled that I would find strength to meet my hardest challenges and fears with words from the great books and looking to *higher ground.*

My challenge to you is to attach yourself to the Vine, the source of peace, strength, confidence, and comfort. "Look unto me in every thought; doubt not, fear not" (Doctrine and Covenants 6:36).

COURAGE TO THE CORE

"Courage to the core gives you courage to Conquer More."

—Trevor Farnes

Since MTN OPS was founded on a set of Core Values and beliefs that we stand firmly planted on, I loved that these were not just fancy words written on the walls of our office. Instead, they were truly written upon the hearts of those working within those walls and embodied inside each of us. Rather than always speaking about these Core Values at MTN OPS, we would prefer that our customers and partners see them being *lived*, truly having the courage to live from the core.

The original Core Values of MTN OPS were assembled at a business I worked at with my brothers from 2002 to 2007. They were so powerful, I carried the precepts and tenets with me. Since starting MTN OPS, however, we have added three additional and the essential core values of Ownership, Diligence, and Joy.

We now have twelve core values, each one assigned to a month in the year for ourselves and our entire team. Each month, the team focuses on, talks about, and receives training on the assigned value. Surprisingly—or perhaps not so—the MTN OPS core values and beliefs reflected values taught in my home in my earliest years of life.

THE MTN OPS MANIFESTO

WE ARE BUILT TO CONQUER MORE

In everything we do we improve the lives of individuals and families. our commitment to you is made manifest through this proclamation. the journey of transformation spiritually, physically, mentally, and socially is a journey to conquer. MTN OPS is your trusted partner.

At the heart of MTN OPS we strive each day to conquer more by abiding by a set of core values and beliefs that will reflect in our interactions, but also in our product and services you have trusted in us to provide. The following is our commitment to you...

We believe in RECOGNIZING GOD, even in the workplace, and acknowledge His hand in all things. The individuals at MTN OPS are mindful and prayerful in considering how we produce products and services that will benefit the human family.

We believe that OWNERSHIP is the essence of leadership. We take full and personal responsibility for our actions and outcomes, especially those that affect our customers. At the end of the day each of us must take responsibility for the outcomes we desire in life. In the words of William Ernest Henley *"I am the master of my fate, I am the captain of my soul."* We challenge you to own the day and the choices that direct you to conquer more in life.

We believe in being worthy of others' TRUST. We are reliable, respectful, and honest with the information we provide to you along with the information you provide to us. We are impeccable with our word. Your journey of transformation can be trusted to MTN OPS.

Our team works together with true INTERDEPENDENCE to accomplish great things collectively that we could not do independently. You are now a part of this incredible MTN OPS FAMILY and we expect each member of the family to play a role in lifting where they stand in our efforts to conquer more.

We commit to DILIGENCE in exerting a constant, earnest and energetic effort to help you conquer your goals.

We foster an atmosphere that gives you and others an OPPORTUNITY to rise to your full potential.

Because we believe FAMILY is the fundamental unit of community, we desire the type of environment that promotes healthy families. All MTN OPS content, events, and experiences will remain FAMILY friendly.

We value highly ambitious people - driven by a DESIRE to succeed but with an attitude of temperance. We will work with you to ambitiously transform your life, all the while realizing that it takes time and patience for results to be achieved. Let's win each day and trust the process.

We believe in making a positive contribution of our time, talents, and leadership through SERVICE to our respective communities. With every one of your orders we have donated a meal to a child in need. Our community has now produced the resources to feed MILLIONS of children all across the country and internationally through our OPERATION CONQUER HUNGER.

We believe in the GOLDEN RULE and in treating you and everyone exactly how we would like to be treated in regard to honesty, responsiveness, follow-through, and in going the extra mile to ensure that your needs and desires are met.

GRATITUDE for both our successes and our challenges helps us have joy in our current circumstances while facilitating our growth and progress toward an even brighter future. We thank you for trusting MTN OPS to support you in your transformational goals.

How happy we are in life has very little to do with the circumstances of our lives and everything to do with the focus of our lives. Amidst all the distractions of daily living, we focus on finding JOY in the journey and invite you to trust in us on this JOURNEY OF JOY.

As a MTN OPS family we welcome you to the life of a conqueror and are with you each step of the way.

Each core value and belief is important to us and is part of the Conquer More Challenge. There is tremendous impact and meaningful change and progress when lived. I will share below what they mean to us. Some I will spend more time on, and others I'll just give a brief explanation, but all are undeniably critical to the success of not only MTN OPS but the individuals lives that are led by these and similar core values and beliefs.

FAMILY

Because we believe family is the fundamental unit of community, we desire the type of environment that promotes healthy families. We work hard and honestly so that we may enjoy a secure life with the ones we love.

"No success can compensate for failure in the home."

–David O. Mckay

I firmly believe that one day, I will be judged by my Creator—but not by the amount of money I made, the kind of car I drove, or the size of the house I lived in. But what I will be held accountable for is how well I did in my roles as husband, father, son, brother, and neighbor. This does not mean it is not important to work toward a successful career or even financial success and security, but none of that will truly matter if we gain the world but lose in the most sacred arenas of our lives.

We are each much more successful and able to contribute in the workplace when all is well at home. The most sacred work we will ever do will be within the walls of our own home. Being able to come to work having contributed in the right way within the walls of our own home will allow for a much greater you with capacity and ability beyond your own.

GRATITUDE

Gratitude for both our successes and our challenges helps us have joy in our current circumstances while facilitating our growth and progress toward an even brighter future.

A friend once asked me on a phone call, "What if you woke up today with only the things you thanked God for yesterday?"

What a profound question.

What would I have today?

Who would you have?

Where is the focus of your life?

Take a minute to stop reading and think to yourself, "What did I thank God for yesterday?" Are the things you are grateful for recognized as you speak to God in prayer each day?

As you go to bed tonight, I challenge you to take three to five minutes or more if you can and kneel at your bedside and pray to God, thanking Him for those things you desire to wake up to tomorrow. Above all else, I am sure your thoughts of gratitude will focus on relationships, health and well-being, and less about temporary, material things.

As part of The Conquer Code, I would challenge you to commit to conquer by writing down those things you are grateful for today in a gratitude journal. I would even challenge you in the stormy phases of life to consider and express gratitude for the lessons being learned and how they can make you stronger in this very moment and in the years to come! Having eyes to see in the middle of the storm and the lessons you have to gain will give you that joy in your *current* circumstances—and I promise it will facilitate your growth and progress toward an even brighter future.

INTERDEPENDENCE

We work with a team to accomplish great things collectively that we could not do independently.

"...in the midst of our afflictions, we found a friend..."

—Joseph Smith -History 1:61

I want to tell you about a friend I found amidst our afflictions. About six months after Jenna and I had started our first supplement company, I needed help. If I wanted to grow this company, I could not continue to do it all on my own. Our accountant at the time mentioned that he had a friend who might be interested in a good opportunity. I wasn't sure if what we had was a "good opportunity" for the caliber of person our accountant's friend was.

From what I had heard, Nick was an up-and-coming golden boy at Goldman Sachs, rising through the ranks in many regards. Shortly after meeting Nick, I could understand why. He was flying home from New York City, where the Goldman Sachs team was trying to convince him to stay with the great opportunity to move to The Big Apple.

Nick agreed to meet with me in our one-office operation. He was young, ambitious, and looking for something he could really get behind and people he could enjoy working with. I came to find that Nick was single, had done well financially, and that if there were a time for him to take a risk, it was now.

I also found that the lack of work-life balance at Goldman was a real factor in Nick's leaving. He told me he even had thoughts going through his head while driving to work that he'd hoped for a car to crash into him on the way, just so he would not have to be in the office that day. I was shocked.

Then I gave Nick an offer he couldn't refuse: ten dollars an hour or his commission, the greater of the two. What I believe caught hold of Nick, more than this irresistible offer, was the opportunity to gain balance in his life. I have been and always will be a huge proponent of truly living. For me, even as a business owner, business has never become my identity. I see business as an asset *in* my life, providing me with resources to do what I am truly meant to do. Fortunately for us, an immediate connection and friendship formed, and we were off to the races.

Immediately, Nick began to carry a load different from mine; he began to call on new customers along with me, and we divided the workload. I had immediate trust in him, which was so important in this interdependent relationship. As his follow-through was impeccable, we were able to rely on each other more and more—and our ability to succeed together began to unfold.

We began to accomplish things I was not able to do on my own. The number of accounts was now growing, so we started advertising a bit more and trying to attend more events. While it was such a humbling experience for me, it was also very empowering. Nick brought no ego with him, so there was no feeling of one being better than another. We both did our part and recognized that in trusting each other to do our part, we found real growth.

Within the first week of working with me, Nick found he had partnered with a young father who had a lot on his plate:

- I had just been called into the bishopric (an ecclesiastical position) in my 500+ church congregation for five years.
- I had just started school.
- Jenna and I had just had our third child.
- I was working long hours to get this business off the ground, and I was broke.

I only mention this because of the kindness Nick extended, the support he always offered, and the friendship that was so needed by me at the time. I know for a fact that he could have quickly run the other way, wondering what he got himself into. He has never said this to me, but I think my family and I became part of Nick's mission, his *why*.

Nick seemed to know that one of the reasons God had caused our paths to cross was that he could help me through the struggle I was in as a father, husband, and business owner. Yet Nick *stayed*!

Nick even provided me with gift cards along the way so that I could take my wife out on anniversary and birthday dinners. One of the things I will always remember about those early days was the lunches he would frequently buy for me. For a few years, if Nick didn't invite me and offer to pay for me, I would simply go without lunch. In fact, I had a brown paper bag at one point.

I will use this bag every day, I thought back then. *I'll bring a home lunch to work, and I will put a tally mark on the bag each day to represent how many home lunches I brought, demonstrating my being helpful with the family budget, which doesn't include lunch money...*

My attempt failed quickly, as we didn't always have something for me to take from home to eat at lunch. So I went most of the days without lunch at all and very few tally marks on the brown bag.

The days Nick took me to lunch were a bright point in my week and life. It felt good to eat good food with a good friend. As I look back at all that has been accomplished with Operation Conquer Hunger, I think of Nick and his willingness to help me conquer my own hunger on a regular basis. Nick had eyes to see and a heart to respond to the needs of another, and I will always be grateful for that.

Leaving the intersection of our office, I was once a few cars behind Nick. There was a homeless family on the corner, and my heart sank as I didn't have any cash to offer. I watched as Nick noticed this family at the last second as he pulled out onto the busy street. It would have been easy for him to just say, "*Oh well, I am out on the busy street now and on my way, I hope they get some help,*" but not Nick. I watched in astonishment as he quickly flipped a U-turn and got back in the lineup of cars. As he got closer to the family, his window rolled down to offer them assistance. I was touched by his caring and generosity, just as I have been each day working with him since.

Not only is working with people important to a team's success, but it is also important to work with the right people. Make sure you work under the same value set or principles as your guiding light and north star. This is how true, impactful, and lasting culture is formed. For years, Nick and I would come together every single morning in prayer for success upon the day.

Our lives and our livelihoods depended upon that success. My family and Nick's future family were our constant focus. This reliance on each other and on God got us through some very difficult years as we struggled to find the right approach and the right message to gain the traction we needed.

Finding the right team that doesn't give up is critical to conquering more. So much of what creates success is just not quitting and sticking to something you feel in your heart to be good. I've seen so many business owners and partnerships quit in the first months or first year of a business because success doesn't happen immediately, and in an attempt to find instant success and gratification, they jump to the next venture

Now, there are those who can't financially withstand the ups and downs, and to no fault of their own, things don't materialize, and change needs to occur. But in many instances, we need to learn to delay our gratification, as hard as it is, and truly sacrifice. Working with all our heart, mind, and strength helps us endure the difficulties that will inevitably arise in building a business.

It is after those moments of grit we have endured that we will more than likely find some form of success. We all hope financial success will follow, but what if mental fortitude, emotional strength, patience, endurance, and faith are the outcome of our efforts? I would say success is achieved.

The sooner you can assemble a team, whether in business or in life, whoever is willing to grin and bear the burdens, the struggles, and the faith required to succeed will be better off. Find your own Nick Hanks who will enhance your ability to achieve. Equally as important is the support that enhances other's abilities to succeed. One thing to remember is that Nick was there supporting me in my dreams, but it was not only my dreams that needed supporting; Nick had dreams, ambitions, and desires to succeed, and I was supporting him as well. When our desires and ambitions were clear to each other and we found the commonality between the two, we were unconquerable.

DESIRE

We value highly ambitious people driven by a desire to succeed but with an attitude of temperance and kindness.

"Desire is the starting point of all achievement, not a hope, not a wish, but a keen pulsating desire which transcends everything."

—Napoleon Hill

There is great power in positive thought combined with consistent and relentless pursuit of the desires of your heart and soul. Right about the time we started the business in 2010, my wife and I read the book *Think and Grow Rich* together. It was a powerful experience, especially looking back upon what transpired. But what I love about looking back is that everything we did, we did together. We had one common goal, one common ambition, one common desire, and at the center of it all resided a faith in God that His ability to bless and watch over us would prevail.

The title of Hill's book is somewhat deceiving; you can't simply think about it and make it happen. That said, the power of positive thinking can propel us forward in the right direction, taking steps toward the right and ultimate destination. I always tell my team at MTN OPS, "The choices you make in the shoes you wear today will determine the shoes you wear tomorrow." So much of that comes down to thought and desire.

In Napoleon Hill's book, Jenna and I learned we needed an "All-Consuming Desire." We knew personally that nothing would give you an all-consuming desire to succeed quite like failure. Having been on the other side of success, I did not want to go back in that direction. The only option was up and out of the deep and dark hole we had found ourselves in. While I always thought of myself as a positive thinker, there was much room for improvement and more consistency, persistence, and a higher ambition to stay positive in my desire.

While reading the book, we followed an exercise to write down our desires. We closed our eyes and visualized our success and what it looked and felt like. We visualized when the success occurred, how it happened, and what we were willing to do to make it a reality.

I grabbed a small piece of paper from my nightstand and, with Jenna's help, we wrote our desires, our goals, and what we were willing to do to make it happen. The next morning, I used tape to laminate our newly created goal sheet. We read this out loud to each other every day for a time to really get it ingrained into our thinking. Now, thirteen years later, I still have that special declaration that states:

- By the end of April 2011, We will be making $___ amount per month.
- By the end of May 2012, $___ amount per month.
- By the end of June 2013, $___ amount plus per month, there on out.
- This money will come to us through our efforts in ___ business.
- In return for this income, I will give the most of all my talents and energy to the job, to my family, to my service, and to my education. I will work with others' interests in mind and
- Always, always remember my GOD from whom all blessings come. He will be my #1 partner, along with my wife.
- I can feel it and see it in my mind. Nothing can stop me. All my previous failures will be met with far greater success.

Now, looking back thirteen years later, everything we had desired and more has come to pass. It is not because we read that book, but because we put into practice the power of positive thinking. We wrote our desires down as if we were already watching them happen, and then we went to work. The power of hard work is incredible. The harder I worked, the more I learned and the more capable I became in the work I was doing. Experience does bring about ability, and the more our desires push us to action, the more experience we gain.

As stated in our description of Desire, we value highly ambitious people driven by a desire to succeed. That ambition and desire is demonstrated by a person's faith and action. True faith requires action. "Faith without works is dead' (James 2:17 KJV). You can pick a person of faith out of a crowd because they show their works in their actions.

The next part of that description says, "With an attitude of temperance." Have you ever seen someone succeeding, and want the world to know all about it? That is not the way of The Conquer Code. Those individuals are rewarded by the world's recognition of their success.

An attitude of temperance doesn't mean we can't celebrate our successes, but it does mean we recognize from whom those successes come, and so we celebrate with humility, gratitude, kindness, and patience. An attitude of temperance brings about a desire in others to join us in our success because it is welcoming, it is kind, and it is motivating.

OPPORTUNITY

We foster an atmosphere that gives others the opportunity to rise to his or her full potential.

"Not knowing when the dawn will come, I open every door."

—Emily Dickinson

We must never feel like our opportunities in life have passed us by. Yes, we might not have taken advantage of opportunities as we should have in the past, but for each of us, a new day is a new opportunity to conquer a little more. It all comes down to our perspective on life and the opportunities of each new day. Where there is a will and a day, there is a way!

I would love to recognize the many individuals who saw MTN OPS as an opportunity, who with all their hearts have dedicated themselves even at this very moment, some in the past, and I look forward to meeting all those who will eventually be a part of our incredible team in the future. These are individuals who have used MTN OPS as a stepping stone in their personal development and growth toward achieving their ultimate potential. I pray a small part of what we add to their lives is as impactful as their lives have been on me.

SERVICE

> **We believe in making a positive contribution of our time, talents, and leadership to our respective communities.**

As an entrepreneur who has had many failed attempts in business, there was often much service rendered to our family. Much of that service came from food and groceries being left on our doorstep, at times by people unknown to us but known to God. Angels who knew precisely what foods and treats our children would love.

One morning, I remember leaving the house and heading to the office. I remember feeling empty as I left Jenna and our children at home with nothing in the pantry. The cupboard was bare, and I felt this burden like I was carrying the world's weight on my shoulders. Not long after I had left, I got a call from Jenna, and with evident emotion in her voice, she said,

"We've had another miracle."

"What is it?" I anxiously asked.

"I put the girls in the tub, went to our closet, knelt, and began to pray that God would give us something today to help us in our struggles. As soon as I said amen in my prayer, the doorbell rang, and as I opened the door, there was a pile full of groceries. The entire porch was full of groceries."

I became emotional at the blessing of this day and the heaven-sent miracle we found on our doorstep.

On this occasion, the Cheez Whiz in the groceries was heaven-sent, and only someone who knew our daughter Hallie would have known how much she loved Cheez Whiz. It was a simple item we could not afford at the time, but you would have thought she struck gold. I thank God daily for those who blessed our family with those necessities of life.

In 2010, Jenna and I were presented with an opportunity to donate twenty-two dollars a month to a foundation that would feed a child in Malawi Africa thirty meals. It was a sacrifice for us, but Jenna and I decided to subscribe to the twenty-two-dollar program that would feed a child. We knew what it was like to go without. We were not starving, but we were hungry, and we wanted to do our part to remove that hunger from the lives of others. I was so grateful for an opportunity to participate in something like this. I felt an energy and an ambition around doing what we could to help hungry children, and not just hungry children, but the parents who were suffering knowing that their children were hungry.

I told Jenna how awesome it would be to build a business that would allow us to feed hungry children. I created marketing slides and tried to strategize a plan to create a business that fed the hungry, but I wasn't exactly sure how to manifest this vision into reality. I was broke and really needed some guidance on which steps to take next in life to provide. Jenna and I loved the scriptures of Jesus speaking to Peter in John 21:

> "'Lovest thou me?'
>
> 'To which Peter replied, 'Thou knowest I love thee.'
>
> 'Jesus responded with a command 'Feed my sheep.'"

We were the sheep being fed by those who loved the Lord during our times of hunger. We knew that the Savior was commanding Peter to feed his sheep with the gospel, but I also listened to this in our time of hunger as a literal command to *feed His sheep*, and I desired to do so.

Another Bible story and miracle we cherish are the moments when Christ took a few loaves and fishes and multiplied them for the thousands. Being touched by these stories through our years of hunger, we committed to each other and to God that once we had just a few loaves and a few fishes, we would dedicate them and work to multiply them for the masses. We wouldn't wait until we had made it financially, or in other words, for our boat to come in full of fish. Our commitment was to take what few loaves and fishes given to us by God and partner with Him to multiply our resources for the masses of children who are suffering from hunger every day.

With this commitment, we continued to make our small donation of twenty-two dollars each month, a payment that was not always easy to pay. But we were committed.

As we began MTN OPS and our mission to improve the lives of individuals and families was defined, we found an opportunity to make our desire a relevant reality. At MTN OPS, we provide people with a way to supplement their nutrition. As hunters and outdoorsmen, we obtain much of our protein and part of our nutrition through the animals that we harvest. I began to see a correlation between this and an opportunity to provide nutrition to those who could never fathom supplementing their nutrition with an even greater cause. That's when Operation Conquer Hunger was born.

The loaves and the fish began to multiply as we donated a meal for every order that came through our website. Oftentimes, we even donated five, ten, or even twenty meals per order, depending on our marketing campaigns and the available resources to do so.

After starting Operation Conquer Hunger, it took us four years to donate our first million meals. But wow! What an accomplishment. Our team and our community were extremely excited. We made the million-meal donation announcement at an Operation Conquer Hunger event that was held at a local school my children attended.

The one million meal donation celebration was actually made on a stage where I once danced in a daddy dance-off at Hallie and Kenzie's dance recital. The only reason I danced was to win the gift card given to the best daddy dancer. It was almost Jenna's birthday, and I had no money to buy her a gift, so I danced my heart out! I won, and because of this, Jenna had a present on her birthday. But now we were dancing for one million meals and multiplying our efforts to bless those in need. What a blessing and a gift.

In 2020, just one week before Covid turned our lives upside down, we held our largest Operation Conquer Hunger event to date as we packed close to sixty thousand meals in just under two hours. The food pantry where these food packs were to be sent was overwhelmed with the quantity and told us they might not be able to accept the full donation.

A few days later however, they told us they felt prompted to find space for the meals and to bring them in despite the lack of space. Within days, the chaos of Covid shook our world and kept kids home from school, but that donation ended up feeding the children of our district during the hardest days of Covid.

In April 2020, we came together as a team once more. In the midst of job loss and skyrocketing unemployment, we increased our donations per order and donated five hundred thousand meals in that month alone. Those meals were donated throughout the country and through partners such as Feeding America. What took us four years to donate (our first million meals) was duplicated in 2020 alone, and we hit two million meals donated through our Operation Conquer Hunger.

In 2021, we donated an additional one million, five hundred meals, and in November 2022, we celebrated a huge milestone of surpassing four million meals donated. Our commitment is resilient and relentless, and in no time, we will hit our goal of five and then ten million meals.

As I write this, I am overwhelmed with gratitude and emotion as I think of the small beginnings, the hunger we faced, the meals donated to us, the loaves and fish we began with, the twenty-two dollar monthly donation to children in Malawi, Africa, and now the millions of meals that have been donated. The Lord truly can and will multiply our efforts and resources, especially for a cause that helps to *feed His sheep*.

What we now pack and deliver to children in need are called Conquer Hunger Pantry Packs. We gather and assemble these packs, and then children receive them from their school principals. The meals we pack include oatmeal, macaroni, ravioli, granola bars, fruit packs, pudding, crackers, milk, juice, and a few other items. Each child also receives a card from us at MTN OPS that reads the words from Winnie the Pooh:

You are braver than you believe
Stronger than you seem
Smarter than you think
Loved more than you know
YOU WERE MADE TO CONQUER

At the end of the day, we are doing much more than filling a belly that needs food. We are inspiring hope, confidence, and a realization within these children that they are loved, seen, cared about, and can do so much in this life. As we remove the distracting hunger, we inspire to Conquer More.

TRUST

We believe in being worthy of others' trust, both in person and online. We are reliable, respectful, and honest with the information we provide to people along with the information they provide to us.

It has been said that trust takes years to build, seconds to break, and forever to repair.

In the Harvard Business Review, an article regarding trust speaks of three elements in business that are at play when creating trust with your team.

The first is *Positive Relationships,* which states, "Trust is in part based on the extent to which a leader is able to create positive relationships with other people."

Second is *Good Judgment/Expertise,* which states, "Another factor in whether people trust a leader is the extent to which a leader is well-informed and knowledgeable. They must understand the technical aspects of the work as well as have a depth of experience."

Third is *Consistency,* which says, "The final element of trust is the extent to which leaders walk their talk and do what they say they will do. People rate a leader high in trust if they: are a role model and set a good example. Walk the talk. Honor commitments and keep promises. Follow through on commitments. Are willing to go above and beyond what needs to be done."

I challenge us to look at every meaningful relationship in life and ask some questions—not just those in business, but within our communities and, most importantly, within our family.

- Do we show up as a positive relationship for those who know us?
- Do we exercise good judgment in how we interact with those around us?
- Do we do what we say we will do, and are we impeccable with our word?

A mentor once asked me to ask myself the following questions:

- What would it be like to work for me?
- What would it be like to be my wife?
- What would it be like to be a child of mine?

Those questions still compel me to be a better human daily. We will always have room to improve, but hopefully, over time, we can build the type of trust with those we work with, those we are married to, and those we are blessed to raise that will enable them to *know us* at our core and not be surprised by our daily actions, routines, responses, and the strength of our follow-through.

GOLDEN RULE

We believe in treating our partners and also our online customers exactly how we would like to be treated in regard to honesty, responsiveness, follow-through, and in going the extra mile to ensure that their needs and desires are met.

Ultimately, I believe that the Golden Rule will mean everything to all of us in the end. But the Golden Rule that is stated above is a little different from what I might describe here now. There is a scripture I love that hit me with great force this last year and reminded me of this *core value* we live but also ties to the core value of *Recognizing God.*

The scripture in Alma 41 verse 14 reads: "Therefore, my son, see that you are merciful unto your brethren; deal justly, judge righteously, and do good continually; and if ye do all these things then shall ye receive your reward; yea, ye shall have mercy restored unto you again; ye shall have justice restored unto you again; ye shall have a righteous judgment restored unto you again; and ye shall have good rewarded unto you again. For that which ye do send out shall return unto you again, and be restored; therefore, the word restoration more fully condemneth the sinner, and justifieth him not at all."

When I read this passage of scripture and applied it to The Golden Rule, the words came to my mind inspired by Jesus's Sermon on the Mount. Often, when I'm working with my team, I share that we should "do unto others as you would have God do unto you." Ultimately, in the end, as we are brought before our maker, it will matter how we treat others, and with the same judgment we have judged, we shall be judged; with the same mercy we extend, we shall receive the good we do to others from our Creator.

Spencer W. Kimball once spoke of our need to treat *all* those we come in contact with as our brothers and sisters. He said: "We must remember that those mortals we meet in parking lots, offices, elevators, and elsewhere are that portion of mankind God has given us to love and to serve." Someone emulated that to me early in raising a family, and I'll never forget it.

As I ponder upon this, my mind races back to the days of our financial struggles. We needed a few things from the store. My wife gave me a short list, which included diapers, wipes, and some milk. That was all we could afford for our three children. Beckham was a newborn; Kenzie was a toddler, and Hallie was just a few years older.

Hallie climbed out of the car and entered the store, holding my hand. We gathered the few items and approached the cash register. I began to shake inside. Going up to the cash register was always a scary thing for me because, in those days, I wasn't always sure if the card would go through.

So, with fear in my heart and not knowing exactly what was in our meager bank account, I placed the items by the register. The attendant was a middle-aged woman with kindness in her eyes.

After the items were rung up, I swiped my card. "Declined." I swiped again. "Declined." Now acting as if I were completely surprised, I tried one last time: "Declined." At this point, there was a line of people behind me, and I muttered to the attendant that there should have been plenty of money to buy these few items.

As I looked at her, she saw me. She knew that the look in my eyes told a different story. She truly had *eyes to see*—to see what? A father desperately struggling to provide, a worn-down and defeated man, and a husband who needed some confidence. I said, "If you can keep these items here, I'll run home and grab some cash and be right back."

She looked at me, then down at Hallie, and back at me. She replied gently, "That's fine, but take the items with you."

I wanted to break down in tears of gratitude right then and there so I could walk away with the groceries in hand, not feeling like all eyes were on me as a failure. Yes, I still needed to pay, but she gave me an opportunity to escape complete humiliation and embarrassment—something I was all too familiar with at this point. Hallie was young, but I shared with her what had happened and how much gratitude and love I felt for that sweet lady in the store.

I loaded Hallie back in the car and drove from the grocery store to our home. I told Jenna what had happened, dug into our coin jar to find enough change to pay for the items, jumped back in the car and went directly to the store. I couldn't wait to come through on my end for this woman's kindness. I wanted her to know I was a man of my word.

When I arrived at the store, she had moved lanes. When I walked up to her, my fist extended full of coins and my heart full of gratitude, she surprised me when she said, "I already took care of it. You go take care of your beautiful family."

I stood there in shock, in complete and utter awe of her loving generosity. I drove home, the coins still clutched in my hand, grateful tears streaming down my face. What an amazing lesson of love I learned that day. *She did unto me. . .* Don't we all need a little help now and again? Aren't we all beggars in some way or another? Don't we all need mercy?

When I leave my house each day, when I interact with a neighbor, friend, or family member, I pray that, like this woman, I will have *eyes to see* and a *Heart like His* to do as I hope He will do unto me in the end.

RECOGNIZING GOD

We believe in involving God, even in the workplace, and acknowledge His hand in all things.

I have saved this core value for the end, it being of the most importance to me. I believe it was this principle being observed by my parents that continues to give me life today. I have to give my parents credit for living in such a way, that now, after fifty years of marriage, generations and thousands of people are blessed because of their desire to *Recognize God.*

As members of the Church of Jesus Christ of Latter-Day Saints, we live a much stricter standard of worship than many other religions regarding

Sabbath day observance. My parents used the following personal experience to share with us as children how vital the Sabbath day was for them, and because it was important to them, it became important to me.

In 1968, my mother was attending Brigham Young University. A friend of hers talked her into becoming a flight attendant and have the opportunity to travel the country. She was thrilled when, one Saturday, she received a phone call requesting she join a flight crew to Washington D.C. As a flight route she had not yet traveled, she accepted the request, knowing she would return to Utah the following Monday.

Upon arriving in Washington D.C. that Saturday night, one of the other attendants let my mother know they had purchased tickets for a tour of D.C. the next day. My mother had never been to D.C., so this would be a great opportunity. But she kindly declined the offer and let them know she would be attending her church's worship services that day. I am sure her seven future children cheered her on from the heavenly sidelines as she made this all-important choice that would give eternal significance to each of our lives.

How could such a simple decision have made a difference to the seven children and now thirty-five grandchildren and three great-grandchildren?

Gary Farnes, my dad, sat in his usual seat in the 16th Street chapel in Washington D.C., in his white shirt and tie that Sunday morning. This was the congregation my dad met with every single Sunday, as he, too, had made a commitment to *Recognize God* and find strength each week through this worship.

At the time, my dad was studying at George Washington University to become a hospital administrator. Dad always tells us, "Never had I seen someone more beautiful than Mary Orton, who walked into the congregation that Sabbath morning." He adds, "Following the service, I sat in a line waiting to meet this new beauty, who every other single man at church that day also seemed to be waiting to meet!"

When they finally shook hands, he knew and she knew they needed to get to know each other more. He invited her over for a steak dinner that night, but she respectfully declined. Like me, he was not to be undone by a challenge. They became pen pals for almost a year, after which my dad proposed. They were married in the Salt Lake City LDS temple and started their forever family in the city of Baltimore, Maryland, where my dad's first job was located.

At MTN OPS, you might know that we unapologetically and boldly recognize God by trying our best to keep the Sabbath day a holy day. I would say for me, personally, this is in great measure due to my parents' story and the blessings of life and connections that have come from their observance of the Sabbath day.

Their story has inspired me throughout my life to keep the Sabbath day a delight and a holy day to observe my relationship and connection to God.

I once had someone ask, "I see you guys close on Sunday. Isn't there great risk in that?" My response was and will always be, "The greater risk is in me not being true to the commitments I have made with my God."

To Recognize God, I will finish my book with one last personal story and pray that in the end, each of those reading my words, and even myself, will *commit to conquer by choosing God.*

A personal experience that occurred with my son when he was about eight or nine years old helps me to understand how important it is never to forget *and always remember.*

Beckham is an awesome little athlete and played a lot of baseball until he was about seven or eight, when he decided to put the bat and mitt away to take up soccer. I grew up playing soccer, and, obviously, my wife and I even named him "Beckham," so needless to say I was very excited when my own son wanted to play the sport I loved so much.

He tried out for a competitive team and made it, which was a very exciting day for us all. It came time for his first game, which was a tournament in Logan, Utah. Our family was the first family there that morning. We were so excited with anticipation for his first game. As the game began, the families sat on one side of the field, with the players and coaches directly across the field from us. Beckham wasn't in the starting lineup, which did not bug me because, after all, this was his first year, first game, and he was the new kid on the team. He sat patiently waiting on the bench, his feet not yet able to touch the ground from where he sat, so his legs swung back and forth as he waited.

About halfway through the first half, the two coaches started subbing players in and out of the game, but not my son. I didn't think much of it, to begin with, but my eyes never left the focus on my son and the coaches. I waited in anticipation for him to be put into the game, but as it neared the end of the first half, I started to feel that they had forgotten him. Some frustration started to set in. Beckham would occasionally look across the field to me, and I would give him thumbs up. He would do thumbs up back and continue to swing his legs, and then the first half ended.

I looked to Jenna and asked if I should go talk to the coaches. She calmed me down and said, "Let's see how it plays out in the second half. It's one game."

Sure enough, the second half started and there sat my son, in the same position on the bench. I sat and watched as he patiently waited for his opportunity. Halfway through the second half the coaches again started to sub kids in and out, but again, not my son. I couldn't understand what was happening.

I had seen my son play and knew he was just as good as the kids on the team, even much better than some. There had to be some mistake, but what? I started to conjure up in my head everything I would say to the coaches after the game: *What lousy and unaware coaches they are! We're going to pull him from the team.*

Again, Beckham looked my way, and I gave him another thumbs up, just to make sure he knew I was aware of him and that he was not forgotten. Oh, how my heart ached for my son. . . Then, right toward the end of the game, there was some commotion on the sideline with the coaches; they looked confused. Suddenly, they called his name! Beckham stood up and was sent to the sideline to be put in the game. As Beckham ran onto the field, one of his coaches yelled, "I apologize, Beckham!" And just about the time he got to the center of the field, the whistle blew, and the game was over.

My heart broke into a million pieces for my son! I wanted to run to him, to rescue him, and to take away any pain and embarrassment he might be feeling. The team huddled on the side of the field and did their cheer, and then Beckham came running across the field to me, with his coach following right behind.

As Beckham got closer, I asked, "Beckham, what happened?"

"I don't know."

Then wrapping his arms around me he said, "But thanks for bringing me, Dad."

What? I thought.

"Thanks for bringing you to a game you didn't play in?" I said loud enough for his coach to hear.

The coach then apologized to both of us, letting us know that each coach thought the other coach was subbing in Beckham's position, and they didn't realize it until the very end. I shared my feelings with the coach in a *kind and loving way* (not as loving as my wife would have liked it), and then it was over.

There I sat, paralyzed in my chair, long after everyone had left the field. I was filled with so much emotion. My wife and kids wanted to go, but I could not move. I could have just stood up and walked to the car, but I recognized a distinct feeling and knew I needed to stay.

Something deep inside me was building up, and I knew I needed to be still, in the moment, and listen to my heart. Amidst my emotions and thoughts, a powerful spiritual experience began to take place, and I felt as though I was being taught a greater lesson from God.

For a moment, I saw and felt what our Heavenly Father might feel when we *forget about His son. . .*

He had to watch and stand by as His Son had been forgotten and treated unfairly. Yet he still gave thanks and, in a similar attitude, told his Father not to worry about those who had forgotten him.

"Forgive them, for they know not what they do." - Luke 23:34 (KJV)

I saw my son who, like many of us, might feel overlooked, forgotten about, wondering when it's his time to shine, to be included, to be blessed, might come.

I saw a coach who, like so many of us, runs to the *Son* and to the Father, asking for forgiveness for lack of oversight and need for improvement.

I recalled times in my past when I felt left alone, forgotten about, and needed to find patience through a trial. A familiar face or feeling from across the field with a friendly thumbs up, keep going, you can do this, encouraged me enough to just hold on and sit tight a little longer, to Conquer More.

As I sat stunned by this experience, four words pierced my heart and engraved themselves in my mind. They came so powerfully and so swiftly that the words replayed themselves in my mind for what felt like an entire month following this experience:

DON'T FORGET MY SON

In the end, when all is said and done, He is ***MY CONQUER CODE!***

As I end this book, full of many stories and experiences, you will find that I have been blessed to conquer through connection. Any amount of success I may have seen or will see in the future comes through a connection to my team, my family, and my God. The original title of my book was going to be How I Conquer, but as the writing progressed over time, I realized that to unlock success with the conquer code truly, it could never be How "I" Conquer, but How "WE" Conquer.

My wife Jenna and I would like to end this book by sharing our witness that Jesus Christ is the author and finisher of our faith. He is the Messiah, the only begotten of the Father, the Savior and Redeemer of the world. He is the strength of our marriage, our home, and our lives. Through a connection and relationship with Him, we can find lasting peace in this life and in the eternities. To all of life's questions, the answer is Jesus Christ.

In moments when we felt we were drowning, like Peter in the New Testament, we have cried out, "Save us," it has always been and will always be Him who is there with His hand stretched out still, all the days of our lives. It will be Him whose feet we wet with our tears when we are reunited with our Savior, our Brother, our Redeemer again. Let this stand as our witness to the world that we believe, know, and testify that Jesus is the Christ and the key to unlocking The Conquer Code.

PHASE 7 CONQUER CHALLENGE

I realize that everyone has their deep-seated belief systems, and I realize that yours might not be the same as mine. Amongst my own friends and family, business collaborators, and others, I am grateful for and deeply aware of different spiritual truths and points of view that are all sacred.

In this section, I challenge you to write down three things that you will do starting today to never forget and always remember about Awakening the Divine inside of you! I shared with you my Conquer Code. Write yours in this section and enjoy the journey as you Conquer More.

EPILOGUE: The Conqueror

I am part of the cause of the conquerors.

The dye has been cast. I have stepped over the line. The decision has been made. I am built to CONQUER.

I won't look back, let up, slow down, or be still.

My past is redeemed, my present makes sense, and my future is in God's hands.

I am finished and done with low living, small planning, smooth knees, colorless dreams, tamed visions, worldly talking, cheap giving, and dwarfed goals.

I no longer need preeminence, positions, promotions, plaudits, or popularity.

I don't have to be right, first, recognized, praised, regarded, or rewarded. I now live by faith, lean on His presence, walk with patience, am uplifted by prayer, and labor with love.

My face is set; my gait is fast; my goal is to conquer more. My road is narrow; my way is rough; my companions are few; my guide is reliable, and my mission is clear.

I cannot be bought, compromised, detoured,
lured away, divided, or delayed.

I will not flinch in the face of sacrifice, hesitate in the presence of adversity, negotiate at the table of the enemy, ponder at the pool of popularity, or meander in the maze of mediocrity.

I won't give up, shut up, let up, or slow up until I have stayed up, stored up, stood up, and paid up for the cause of the conqueror.

I must go till I can't, give till I drop, share till all know, and work till I'm stopped. And when you measure my life it will be clear:

I AM A CONQUEROR.

—AUTHOR UNKNOWN

ACKNOWLEDGMENTS

I want to thank those who have been alongside me on this journey. I have mentioned some names throughout the book, but so many incredible people have played a major role in my progress as a conqueror in life, and there is no way I could possibly list them all. I trust that you know who you are, and I pray that you know how grateful I am for each of you.

I have found that in all aspects of life, the learning process is never over, and I am just scratching the surface of learning what it is and what it takes to be a conqueror. With that said, there will be many more people along the way who will lead and lift me as I go. Isn't that what life is all about? They rise highest who lift as they go, and I have many of you to thank for lifting me along the way.

To my MTN OPS team, thank you to all who have ever been a part of the growth of this incredible brand. I share my deepest gratitude for each of you who have been integral to our journey in building this business. Your unwavering support, dedication, hard work, and adherence to the core values of MTN OPS have been instrumental in our success. To those in the very beginning, to everyone actively participating in building the brand today, none of this would be possible without you. Together, we have overcome challenges, celebrated victories, and created a thriving business that is transforming and improving the lives of individuals and families.

To my parents, who laid a solid foundation of love, togetherness, and faith. Your faith has genuinely lit the fire of my faith, and it burns bright today because of you. To my father, who inspired the first product and continues to inspire me today from the heavenly grandstand, I am proud to be your son and will look to the clouds regularly to know, see, and feel your love. To my mother, who has spent her days serving those she loves most, thank you for your dedication to family, finding joy in our journey, and creating a bond that is Together Forever.

To those I dedicate this book to: my wife, Jenna, to my children, Hallie, Kenzie, Beckham, and Savvy, and to my future grandchildren, you are the JOY in my journey. I am nothing without you. To my children, I am so proud to be your father. Your faith inspires me each day. Your love keeps me moving forward. Your future is bright, and the best is yet to come. To my wife, Jenna, you are simply amazing. You are a gift beyond any price. You are my best friend. Your life and the story you have lived inspire me daily. You, indeed, are a conqueror in every sense of the word. Being by your side yesterday, today, and forever is the greatest blessing of my life. You're beautiful beyond anything I ever dreamt of being blessed with. I can't wait to see all that we conquer together. I love my path, but I gain more excitement in many ways, watching my wife and children along their journey and life path. Each of you makes my journey one of excitement, joy, and complete happiness. For you to find and awaken the divine within you on your path is my greatest desire, as I know finding the divine is the hunt of a lifetime.

REFERENCES

- There's an old Hindu legend

  https://hinduism.stackexchange.com/questions/27665/what-did-humans-do-that-brahma-took-away-their-divinity

- The Family – A Proclamation To The World

  https://www.churchofjesuschrist.org/study/scriptures/the-family-a-proclamation-to-the-world/the-family-a-proclamation-to-the-world?lang=eng [KH1]

- *Aspire: Discovering Your Purpose Through the Power of Words*[KH1]
- *Essentialism.*[KH1]
- Robert D. Hales, [KH1] with the sage advice that couples should always focus on three simple phrases: "I love you, I'm sorry, please forgive me."

  https://www.churchofjesuschrist.org/study/general-conference/2004/04/with-all-the-feeling-of-a-tender-parent-a-message-of-hope-to-families?lang=eng

- A therapist in Hawaii realized the power of his thoughts when it came to how he was observing his own patients. He utilized the healing power of a similar Hawaiian phrase called *Ho'oponopono*, and by using it, he healed an entire ward of mentally ill inmates. That Hawaiian therapist was Dr. Ihaleakala Hew Len, and he realized that as humans, we often create our own reality in our thoughts. To be 100 percent responsible for our own lives, we need to change our perception of ourselves—which changes the world and creates miracles. This four-step process is what *Ho'oponopono* literally means:[KH1]

https://hooponoponomiracle.com/iloveyou-imsorry-pleaseforgiveme-thankyou-mantra/

- Father's day video created by The Church of Jesus Christ of Latter-Day Saints

  https://www.churchofjesuschrist.org/media/video/2013-01-0002-earthly-father-heavenly-father?lang=eng

- Malchy McCourt who said, "Resentment is like taking poison and waiting for the other person to die." [KH1]

  https://www.goodreads.com/author/quotes/3373.Malachy_McCourt

- by Doctor Louis Ignarro , who won the Nobel prize in 1998 for his work with nitric oxide as a signaling molecule in the cardiovascular system

  https://www.nobelprize.org/prizes/medicine/1998/ignarro/facts/

- *"Life is not measured by the number of breaths you take, but by the moments that take your breath away." —Maya Angelou*

  https://themindsjournal.com/quotes/life-is-not-measured-by-the-number-of-breaths/

- Russel M. Nelson states "The JOY we feel in life has little to do with the circumstances of our lives and everything to do with the FOCUS of our lives."

  https://www.churchofjesuschrist.org/study/general-conference/2016/10/joy-and-spiritual-survival?lang=eng

- From the words of Russell Bruson, "What if everything you're going through is preparing you for what you asked for?" [KH1]

  https://rethinkquotes.com/russell-brunson-quotes/

- *"It's a dangerous business, Frodo, going out your door. You step onto the road, and if you don't keep your feet, there's no knowing where you might be swept off to." —J.R.R. Tolkien, The Lord of the Rings*

  https://www.goodreads.com/quotes/137661-it-s-a-dangerous-business-frodo-going-out-your-door-you

- According to the Canadian Mental Health Association, "Social connection can lower anxiety and depression, help us regulate our emotions, lead to higher self-esteem and empathy, and actually improve our immune systems."[

  https://cmha.ca/news/the-importance-of-human-connection/

- Jim Rohn once said, "You are the average of the five people you spend the most time with."

  https://www.merakilane.com/90-jim-rohn-quotes-that-promote-personal-development/

- *"Desire is the starting point of all achievement, not a hope, not a wish, but a keen pulsating desire which transcends everything." —Napoleon Hill*

  https://www.goodreads.com/quotes/157262-desire-is-the-starting-point-of-all-achievement-not-a

- *"Not knowing when the dawn will come I open every door." —Emily Dickinson[KH1]*

  https://www.goodreads.com/quotes/125481-not-knowing-when-the-dawn-will-come-i-open-every

- In the Harvard Business Review, an article regarding trust speaks of three elements in business that are at play when creating trust with your team. [KH1]

  https://hbr.org/2019/02/the-3-elements-of-trust

- Spencer W. Kimball once spoke of our need to treat *all* those we come in contact with as our brothers and sisters. He said: "We must remember that those mortals we meet in parking lots, offices, elevators, and elsewhere are that portion of mankind God has given us to love and to serve." [KH1]

  https://www.churchofjesuschrist.org/study/general-conference/2014/04/love-the-essence-of-the-gospel?lang=eng